Coaching for Diversity, Equity, Inclusion, Accessibility, and Belonging in Early Childhood

A Step-by-Step Guide for Programs and Schools

by

Anni K. Reinking, Ed.D.
Reinking Education Consulting, LLC
Peoria, IL

and

Laycee Thigpen, MS.Ed.
Reinking Education Consulting, LLC
Peoria, IL

Baltimore • London • Sydney

Paul H. Brookes Publishing Co.
Post Office Box 10624
Baltimore, Maryland 21285-0624
USA

www.brookespublishing.com

Copyright © 2023 by Paul H. Brookes Publishing Co., Inc.
All rights reserved.

"Paul H. Brookes Publishing Co." is a registered trademark of
Paul H. Brookes Publishing Co., Inc.

Typeset by Absolute Service, Inc., Towson, Maryland.
Manufactured in the United States of America by
Integrated Books International, Inc., Dulles, Virginia.

The individuals described in this book are composites or real people whose situations are masked and are based on the authors' experiences. In all instances, names and identifying details have been changed to protect confidentiality.

Purchasers of *Coaching for Diversity, Equity, Inclusion, Accessibility, and Belonging in Early Childhood: A Step-by-Step Guide for Programs and Schools* are granted permission to download, print, and photocopy the Appendixes in the text for professional purposes. These forms may not be reproduced to generate revenue for any program or individual. Photocopies may only be made from an original book. *Unauthorized use beyond this privilege may be prosecutable under federal law.* You will see the copyright protection notice at the bottom of each photocopiable page.

Library of Congress Cataloging-in-Publication Data

Names: Reinking, Anni K., 1985- author. | Thigpen, Laycee, author.
Title: Coaching for diversity, equity, inclusion, accessibility, and belonging in early childhood : a step-by-step guide for programs and schools / by Anni K. Reinking, Ed.D., Reinking Education Consulting, LLC, Peoria, IL and Laycee Thigpen, MS.Ed., Reinking Education Consulting, LLC, Peoria, IL.
Description: Baltimore, Maryland : Paul H. Brookes Publishing Co., [2023] | Includes bibliographical references and index.
Identifiers: LCCN 2023000814 (print) | LCCN 2023000815 (ebook) | ISBN 9781681256870 (paperback) | ISBN 9781681256887 (epub) | ISBN 9781681256894 (pdf)
Subjects: LCSH: Mentoring in education--United States. | Early childhood education--United States. | Communication in education--United States. | Educational equalization--United States. | Inclusive education--United States. | Belonging (Social psychology) in children--United States. | Educational leadership--United States. | School improvement programs--United States. | BISAC: EDUCATION / Professional Development
Classification: LCC LB1731.4 .R44 2023 (print) | LCC LB1731.4 (ebook) | DDC 371.102--dc23/eng/20230110
LC record available at https://lccn.loc.gov/2023000814
LC ebook record available at https://lccn.loc.gov/2023000815

British Library Cataloguing in Publication data are available from the British Library.

2027 2026 2025 2024 2023

10   9   8   7   6   5   4   3   2   1

Contents

About the Downloads vi
About the Authors vii
Preface viii
Acknowledgments xv

I	Background on DEIAB for EI/ECE 1
1	Diversity, Equity, Inclusion, Access, and Belonging 3
	Definitions 5
	Myths of Equity 17
2	Purposeful Language to Coach and Lead 19
	Purposeful Language Around Identity 20
	Intersectionality 26
	Subjective Versus Objective Language 27
3	Communicating Through Discomfort 29
	Emotional Intelligence 30
	Kind Versus Nice 31
	Hindering Communication 32
	Active Listening 37
	Using Communication to Make Progress 38
II	The Role and Challenges of Coaches and Leaders in Addressing DEIAB Transformation 43
4	Importance of Coaching and Supervising 45
	Coaching 49
	Supervising 51
	Setting Professional Development Goals 52

5	Planning to Start the Work	59
	Planning	59
	Anti-Ism Scale	60
	Coaching to the Anti-Ism Scale	73

III A Guide for Designing an Effective, Transformative DEIAB Program ... 75

6	Designing the Agenda	77
	Writing Workshop Objectives	78
	Whole-Group Learning Topics	80
7	Initial Group Learning	87
	Morning Meeting	87
	Community Agreements	90
	Define Your Why	91
	Concluding the Meeting	92
	The Next Steps	94
8	Equity and Diversity Workgroup	97
	What Is Needed for a Diversity Workgroup?	97
	Benefits of a Diverse Workgroup	99
	Positive Group Dynamics	99
	Barriers to Creating a Diverse Workgroup	100
	Planning for Programmatic Changes	102
	Establishing a Purpose and Statement	103
	Anti-Ism Scale Organization Rating	105
	Setting Goals	106
9	Program Integration	111
	Program Integration Plan	111
	Inevitable Program Pushback	113
	Educating the Educator	114
	Next Steps: Continuing to Learn	115
	Affinity Groups	119
	Book Studies	121
10	Structural (Transformative) Change	123
	Multicultural Curriculum Implementation	123
	Transformative or Structural Change	126
	Outside the Classroom	130
11	Implications for Wider Change	133
	Community Mapping: Strengths, Weaknesses, Opportunities, and Threats	135
	Illinois Case Study	137

12	Epilogue: Keep the Momentum Going	139
	Moving Forward With Administrator Support	142
	Climbing the Mountainside	144

References 145

Appendixes

A	Professional and Organization Criteria Checklist	150
B	Professional Learning Goals Documentation	154
C	Environmental Scan Scoring Guide	155

Index 156

About the Downloads

Purchasers of this book may download, print, and/or photocopy the Appendixes for professional use.

To access the materials that come with this book:

1. Go to the Brookes Download Hub: http://downloads.brookespublishing.com
2. Register to create an account (or log in with an existing account).
3. Filter or search for the book title *Coaching for Diversity, Equity, Inclusion, Accessibility, and Belonging in Early Childhood: A Step-by-Step Guide for Programs and Schools*.

About the Authors

Anni K. Reinking, Ed.D., Owner and Lead Consultant, Reinking Education Consulting, LLC, Peoria, IL

Dr. Reinking is an educator, author, researcher, mother, wife, aunt, daughter, stepmother, social justice advocate, and current elected official (school board member). She has been in the field of education for more than 16 years. As a classroom teacher, she taught in Mombasa, Kenya, the Southside of Chicago, Northwest Indiana, and Central Illinois. Upon leaving the PK–5 classroom learning environment, she worked in the social service field, as a college professor, and as a professional development provider. Furthermore, Dr. Reinking owns Reinking Education Consulting, LLC (www.akreinking.com). In this work, she focuses on facilitating the growth of organizations and schools to increase equity and diversity and to transform them to be places of inclusion.

Laycee Thigpen, MS.Ed., Consultant, Reinking Education Consulting, LLC, Peoria, IL

Mrs. Thigpen is an education consultant, poet, and researcher. She focuses her work on developing racially inclusive environments for early childhood students, families, and educators and combating biases and stereotypes in early childhood classrooms. Mrs. Thigpen has years of experience teaching in child care and Head Start; directing a summer program; and being a supervisor, instructor, and coach for both preservice and in-service teachers. Mrs. Thigpen continues to challenge and motivate educators to establish environments where all people are valued and uses her poetry for reflection in diversity, equity, inclusion, access, and belonging (DEIAB) training. She currently lives in Central Florida with her husband and four children.

Preface

Because you have opened this book, you may be starting your own growth journey, identify as a social justice educator, or fall somewhere in between. Wherever you are in your equity-focused learning journey, we welcome you to this brave space of learning, reading, and reflecting.

We are the authors of this book: Dr. Anni K. Reinking and Laycee Thigpen, MS.Ed. We are self-identified social justice advocates and have been in the education research field focused on diversity since the early 2000s.

We met in 2017 at Southern Illinois University Edwardsville. Dr. Reinking was Mrs. Thigpen's professor in the early childhood program. Since 2019, when Mrs. Thigpen graduated, we have worked continuously to coach, guide, facilitate, and advocate for diversity, equity, inclusion, access, and belonging (DEIAB) at the early childhood level, which lead to transformative, justice-focused learning environments. Through our work, we have continued to push each other to learn, grow, and view the world through different lenses.

We were asked to write this book as a way to share our knowledge regarding the work we do that focuses on educating programs to build equitable environments for all students, families, and educators. As the preschool population becomes more diverse, educational organizations must address the embedded, historically inequitable practices and policies to meet the needs of the inevitable diversity in every community in the United States. There is diversity of thought, diversity of race/ethnicity, diversity of socioeconomics, diversity of sexuality and gender, diversity of religion, diversity of ability, diversity of age, and diversity of experiences. Each of these diverse identities has been, and continues to be, part of early learning environments. Therefore, it is imperative to do this work and to start or continue the conversations regarding transforming early childhood environments to be inclusive for all.

Overall, the information in this book will provide a how-to model filled with reflection questions, activities, and resources, with the overarching theme of DEIAB. Regardless of how "inclusive" your organization believes it is, desires to be, or actually is, this book will serve as a guide. This guide was designed to give early childhood administrators, directors, curriculum coaches, and school leaders a step-by-step process for launching or improving DEIAB work in a program or school. This book connects the knowledge that is often presented in DEIAB trainings with concrete action steps that lead to a transformative environment.

This guide is most effective when used to reflect and acknowledge internal pushback and possibly external pushback from colleagues, families, or administrators, as well as acknowledge the hard work of those on their own equity journey. On this journey, it is important that we recognize the "truth" we were taught and possibly start to relearn the truth and historical contexts of our country—all of which can be challenging. Our hope is that you, as the leader, keep reading and reflecting to eventually question unfair policies and help build a school community that supports all students, families, and educators.

Whether you are novice, advanced, or somewhere in between within the DEIAB field, our challenge to you is to consider the practices, ideas, and identities presented in this book from a beginner's mindset. Everyone has more to learn; however, learning only happens when a person is open to learning. We have continued to learn throughout this process and acknowledge we have more learning to do. So, prepare to start or continue your journey of learning, as we continue ours.

We hope that by reading this book, you, as a leader or coach in the early childhood field, will be able to grow and become better equipped to assist others as they grow and learn within the equity field. Together, with your guidance and this book (and lots of reflection), your organization or the organizations you work with will begin (or continue) to transform into places that acknowledge and value the diversity of families, students, and educators and take the leap from tiptoeing around diversity to inviting it in.

HOW TO USE THIS BOOK

We suggest using this book in one of two ways. First, while reading and reflecting, contextualize the information within theories. There are theories and approaches associated with DEIAB within the education and psychology field that are excellent to ground this work. Second, there is a case study provided throughout the book as a way to see how the practices are applied in real-life situations. Throughout this book, you will witness Program Apples make steps and missteps as they use the guide to become a more equitable environment. Use the case study to see the work in action and reflect on the experiences. In addition, throughout this book, we will walk through the steps of creating an equity-focused early childhood learning environment.

1. Assess the current status of your organization using the Anti-Ism Scale.
2. Plan the work to move forward based on the organization's assessment.

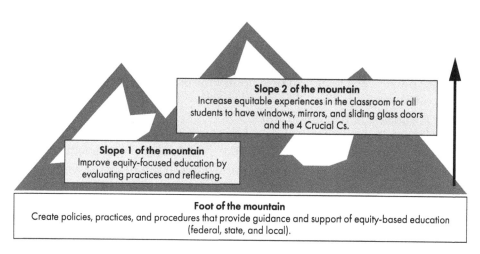

Figure 1. The DEIAB trajectory.

3. Implement the plan through various avenues such as creating a Diversity Workgroup, professional development opportunities, and book studies.

4. Reassess/reflect on the work for continued growth and development.

Finally, we are all moving up a mountain of learning, changing, and reflecting on our own individual journeys. Although you will see the image in Figure 1 again in the last chapter, we provide it here as a primer for the work we will be engaging in throughout this book, as well as beyond your time interacting with the words on the pages of this knowledge-sharing endeavor.

In the remainder of the Preface, we introduce overarching theories and concepts that are foundational pieces of knowledge needed for reading further.

THEORIES

Common theories associated with equity-focused transformations revolve around identities and how the human brain associates similar identities compared to dissimilar identities. Although we do not provide an exhaustive list of theories, we do provide these theories as a way to introduce the context of equity-focused work through the lens of various theories. The descriptions of the theories presented are a starting point for your reflection and further discovery. It is also important to note that many of these theories do not have to stand alone but can be combined in understanding reality.

Critical theories are grounded in two original theories: social identity theory and schema theory. The social identity theory was introduced by Tajfel and Turner in 1986 and is based on the physical, social, and mental characteristics of an individual. Essentially, Tajfel and Turner (1979) proposed that a person's identity group is connected to their sense of self and self-esteem. This then provides the individual with a sense of belonging in the wider social world. For example, if you identify as a White basketball player, both descriptors (White and basketball player) are part of your identity and impact your self-esteem and association with the wider world. Essentially, the social identity theory is based on the concept of identities that are the basis of stereotyping individuals into similarities and differences. This overall concept results in people being grouped in in-groups (us) and out-groups (them).

The concept of grouping individuals into us (in-group) and them (out-group) is also based on the schema theory, which is a branch of cognitive science. Specifically, the schema theory is "concerned with how the brain structures knowledge" (Pankin, 2013, para. 1), which then influences our cognition and behavior. For example, if you always associate tall people as being basketball players, you will unconsciously categorize other tall people as basketball players upon seeing them or meeting them for the first time, regardless of whether they are actually basketball players. What is happening is the process of placing a tall person in the "file" or schema in your brain of tall equals basketball player. This then influences how you interact with tall people, which may include asking about what position they play on the basketball team or whether they have a good jump shot. The process of placing people into our cognitive filing cabinets (folders) is an implicit cognitive impulse; however, that does not provide an excuse for exclusionary practices.

Finally, critical race theory (CRT), which the schema theory and social identity theory are grounded in, was coined by Harvard professor Dr. Derrick Bell in the 1980s to focus on race equity (Ford & Airhihenbuwa, 2009). Essentially, CRT is a way to identify, analyze, and transform societal and institutional structures and cultural aspects that maintain power and oppression of BIPOC+ (Black, indigenous, people of color) individuals (Solorzano, 1997). Simply put, CRT critically analyzes structural and institutional racism to provide guidance for transformation that creates equity. Furthermore, CRT challenges the traditional claims of various social institutions, including education, that operate from "objectivity, meritocracy, color-blindness, race neutrality and equal opportunity" (Solorzano, 1997, p. 6). This means that CRT does not accept the answer of "because it has always been done this way" to explain policies and procedures that further oppress historically marginalized individuals and/or groups.

Branching from CRT, there are two theories that are often cited in the context of gender and sexuality: queer theory and feminist theory.

Queer theory is defined in the Merriam-Webster dictionary as "an approach to literary and cultural study that rejects traditional categories of gender and sexuality." It emerged as a way to dismantle traditional assumptions about gender and sexual identities, such as what it means to be a boy or a girl. Queer theory is grounded in the concept that gender and sexuality are socially constructed ideas that are embedded into humans through socialization (Indiana University, 2021).

According to Ferber and Nelson (2009, p. 1), feminist theory "explores the links between the social construction of scientific disciplines and the social construction of gender, to suggest reasons why differences in experience should not be dismissed as just 'historical digressions.'" Overall, the purpose of feminist theory is to focus on the status of women in society to help improve women's lives, such as providing equal pay.

A final theory to investigate is the critical disability theory, which is "rooted in a critique of traditional discourses and assumptions of disability, which serve to oppress persons with disabilities and infringe on their human rights" (Gillies, 2014, para. 1). The foundation of critical disability theory was built on the premise of power and oppression, much like the other theories described. Therefore, according to Gillies (2014, para. 1), this theory "challenges able-bodied supremacy and the oppression that arises from restricting economic and social benefits to persons with disability which are then redistributed as privileges to be negotiated."

Again, the theories described are not an exhaustive list but will help to start discourse and further investigation. When researching these theories, as well as others, it is important to think about them in the context of DEIAB: diversity (differences), equity (open-mindedness), inclusion (nonexclusionary), access (accessibility), and belonging (affinity).

> **REFLECTION**
>
> How do the theories described, or other theories you find in your research, support the concepts of DEIAB?

ANTIBIAS EDUCATION

According to Teaching for Change (2022, para. 1), antibias education (ABE) is "an approach to early childhood education that sets forth values-based principles and methodology in support of respecting and embracing differences and acting against bias and unfairness. Anti-bias teaching requires critical thinking and problem solving by both children and adults." Derman-Sparks (1989) coined the term and designed the foundational aspects of ABE based on the concept that "young children are aware that color, language, gender, and physical ability are connected to privilege and power. Racism and sexism have a profound influence on children's developing sense of self and others" (p. 161). Therefore, ABE focuses on the assets of each student while also helping students to understand differences and develop a sense of self in relation to the world around them. The four goals of ABE are as follows:

1. Each student will demonstrate self-awareness, confidence, family pride, and positive social identities.
2. Each student will express comfort and joy with human diversity; accurate language for human differences; and deep, caring human connections.
3. Each student will increasingly recognize unfairness, have language to describe unfairness, and understand that unfairness hurts.
4. Each student will demonstrate empowerment and the skills to act, with others or alone, against prejudice and/or discriminatory actions.

Specifically, as Derman-Sparks and Edwards (2010) stated:

> Anti-bias teachers are committed to the principle that every child deserves to develop to his or her fullest potential. Anti-bias work provides teachers a way to examine and transform their understanding of children's lives and also do self-reflective work to more deeply understand their own lives. (p. 2)

The overall goal of ABE is to build students, families, and educators who can confront and eliminate barriers of prejudice, misinformation, and bias about specific aspects of personal and social identity (Teaching for Change, 2022).

At the core of ABE is teaching and reflecting on the concepts of DEIAB. A great way to start the personal reflection when implementing ABE is to move through the following five activities:

- Increase your awareness and understanding of your own individual and social identities in their many facets (e.g., race, ethnicity, gender, ability, sexual orientation, family structure, economic class) and your own cultural contexts, both in your childhood and currently.
- Examine what you have learned about differences, connection, and what you enjoy or fear across all aspects of human diversity.
- Identify how you have been advantaged or disadvantaged by the -isms (e.g., ableism, classism, heterosexism, racism, sexism), and identify the stereotypes or prejudices you have absorbed about yourself or others.
- Explore your ideas, feelings, and experiences regarding social justice activism. Begin a dialogue with colleagues and families about all of these goals.
- Develop the courage and commitment to model for young children that you stand for fairness and as an activist voice for children.

PROGRAM CASE STUDY: PROGRAM APPLES

Throughout the book, we refer to a case study of a real program with the pseudonym "Program Apples." The purpose of using a pseudo-fictional early childhood program is to provide context, examples, and realistic descriptions of the work that is described throughout the book.

For background, Program Apples is a prekindergarten program we have worked with for more than 2 years. The program is located in the southern Midwest and serves 850 preschool students across 10 cities or towns. In addition, they serve around 50 families with infants and toddlers in those same cities and towns. Essentially, this large preschool program covers one entire county, excluding a large metropolitan area, which has their own early childhood program. For children to qualify for this prekindergarten program, they are assessed using an "at-risk" assessment that is utilized within their state. Although they are one program, with one overall work culture and environment, they have the unique advantage that each school and community within their program has its own unique identity. The one unifying statement or mindset among this group of educators, which was often vocalized, was: "We have no diversity. We have all-White kids, so why do we need to learn about this and change?"

We were brought in to help integrate, and ultimately transform, the structure of the program to be more inclusive as a program overall. With the support of the leadership in the program, we worked with staff to guide transformational growth. Our end goal was to empower the educators in the program to guide the work of transformation and accountability.

REFERENCES

Derman-Sparkes, L. (1989). *Anti-bias curriculum: Tools for empowering young children* (pp. 1–5, 11–13). National Association for the Education of Young Children.

Derman-Sparks, L., & Edwards, J. O. (2010). *Anti-bias education for young children and ourselves.* National Association for the Education of Young Children.

Ferber, M. A., & Nelson, J. A. (Eds.). (2009). *Beyond economic man: Feminist theory and economics.* University of Chicago Press.

Ford, C. L., & Airhihenbuwa, C. O. (2009). Critical race theory, race equity, and public health: Toward antiracism praxis. *American Journal of Public Health, 100*(S1), S30–S35. https://doi.org/10.2105/ajph.2009.171058

Gillies J. (2014). Critical disability theory. In A. C. Michalos (Ed.), *Encyclopedia of quality of life and well-being research.* Springer. https://link.springer.com/referenceworkentry/10.1007/978-94-007-0753-5_619

Indiana University. (2021). *Library research guides: Philosophy: Introduction to queer theory.* https://guides.libraries.indiana.edu/c.php?g=995240&p=8361766

Pankin, J. (2013). *Schema theory.* http://web.mit.edu/pankin/www/Schema_Theory_and_Concept_Formation.pdf

Solorzano, D. G. (1997). Images and words that wound: Critical race theory, racial stereotyping, and teacher education. *Teacher Education Quarterly, 24*(3), 5–19. http://www.jstor.org/stable/23478088

Tajfel, H., & Turner, J. C. (1979). An integrative theory of intergroup conflict. In W. G. Austin & S. Worchel (Eds.), *The social psychology of intergroup relations* (pp. 33–37). Brooks/Cole.

Teaching for Change. (2022). *Anti-bias education.* https://www.teachingforchange.org/educator-resources/anti-bias-education

Acknowledgments

From Anni: To my husband (Doug), children (Ahmad, Evie, and Livie), parents (Sue and Frosty), and friends—you are my rock and roots, and I am so thankful for your support. You support my dreams and aspirations through your tireless assistance and conversations, acceptance of my late-night hours, and willingness to binge-watch shows when I need a break.

Laycee, thank you for your willingness to take the professional journey with me. I love how we continue to push, question, and critique each other. Knowing you has made me a better human.

From Laycee: I am grateful for my family. To my husband, Michael, your love and support push me to keep going. To my children, Maya, Michael, Leslie, and Loren, I do this work because of my love for you and children like you. To my parents, I love you and thank you for all of your sacrifices. Thank you to my big sister Toya for always being you and sharing a laugh with me. To my siblings and extended family, I love you all.

Thanks to my best friend, Evan, my friends, and my Shining Light MB Church village, who always have been there and support my big dreams.

Anni, thank you for your friendship and for being willing to grow with me. I appreciate you and your mind.

Thanks are owed to the Southern Illinois University Edwardsville early childhood education professors who helped shape me as a student but also walked beside me as a colleague. Dr. Sherwood and Dr. Swartz, you two have become my friends.

And finally, from both of us: To all early childhood educators, we need you. Stay encouraged.

I

Background on DEIAB for EI/ECE

1

Diversity, Equity, Inclusion, Access, and Belonging

"The history of America is built on the exclusion of certain groups of people, which is grounded in the power and oppression people are born into. However, this historical reality is often unaddressed and ignored in early childhood learning environments."

—Reinking and Thigpen

Whoa! You may be thinking, "This book is not for me if it starts with a statement like that!" Or, you may be thinking, "This book is going to speak truth to power and support my professional growth and learning." Regardless of your initial reaction to the first sentence of this book, you chose to open the book after reading the title. Therefore, yes, this book is for you. This book is for you on your own journey of learning and creating an inclusive classroom.

Throughout the book, we will use the analogy of walking, struggling, and racing up a mountainside to describe each of our learning journeys. On this mountainside, there are several paths, obstacles, and slippery slopes on our independent but sometimes collective and interconnected journey to the summit. The goal of this journey is to reach the point of transformative inclusive practices that focus on equity, access, and belonging for all children and families.

Will we ever reach the summit? No, because there is never a point we will not be learning. Will we all take the same path? No, because we all come with our own experiences and learn in different ways.

On our independent, sometimes winding and intersecting journeys, will we learn and strive for the summit? Our hope is yes!

Therefore, we encourage you to keep reading, discovering, and traveling along your path up the mountainside. Although we will not summit, we all will be somewhere on the side (and hopefully closer to the top) of our transformative mountain through our learning journey, which truly lasts a lifetime.

Where to begin? We must know our past in order to influence our future. So, let's begin by reviewing the history of America.

The history of America is built on exclusion, oppression, power, and privilege; however, this reality is often hidden in the lessons and conversations that occur in early childhood classrooms. Many early childhood professionals believe that young children are not ready for conversations surrounding the isms that America is built on, such as racism, sexism, ageism, and heterosexism. Isms are distinctive beliefs, theories, systems, or practices that are based on exclusionary, prejudiced practices.

Although many early childhood educators might believe that 3-, 4-, and 5-year-old children are too young to discuss isms, we believe children are ready. Research shows that infants as young as 6 months old can show a preference for an individual's skin color. In addition, infants can tell the difference between the sounds and intonations of voices, specifically the use of "motherese" (i.e., baby talk). This ability to differentiate based on environmental cues (visual and auditory) supports the idea that as humans we focus on surviving. We were built as a species to survive; therefore, we pay attention to differences and similarities in our environment. We pay attention to who is in our in-group and who is in our out-group. And evolutionarily, "different" has often been synonymous with "dangerous." (However, today, we know that different does not necessarily mean dangerous, but we must work against our initial reactions and assumptions.)

As Evelyn Green stated in a podcast focused on antibias education (Green et al., 2021), "We have so many things on television. Just take George Floyd for instance. I don't know why people try to pretend that 3-, 4-, and 5-year-olds don't know what is going on in the world." Children know what is going on. They see it, they hear it, and if adults do not provide an explanation to children in developmentally appropriate language, children's imagination can expand beyond reality into something that may seem scary or threatening. So, what is developmentally appropriate for conversations about isms?

Throughout this book, there will be many examples of developmentally appropriate conversations; however, at the core of all of these concepts are the simple ideas of fairness and empathy. Essentially, as the WGBH Educational Foundation (2014, para. 1) explains:

> Children need to learn about fairness and recognize how and when being unfair is hurtful. This lays a foundation for developing empathy and sensitivity that will, in turn, help prevent bullying. But fairness can be a difficult concept for very young children because it is abstract. Young children are often egocentric thinkers, and tend to see the world from their own perspective.

DEFINITIONS

Grounding ourselves in the definitions of diversity, equity, inclusion, access, and belonging will create stepping stones on our own paths up the mountain. In addition, providing definitions will ground you, as a reader and learner, in a common language for moving toward change and possibly cognitive dissonance, which is a good uncomfortable place to land in this work.

Identity (Social)

Some of our social identity attributes are highly visible, such as physical abilities or skin tone, and often collected by schools and other government organizations for reporting purposes. However, there are other attributes that are invisible but claimed by the individual as an identity, such as sexual orientation. As humans, we have a tendency to want to organize or categorize people by their identities, which are often based on social groups, such as race, ethnicity, gender, sex, sexual orientation, religion, socioeconomic status, physical/emotional developmental (dis)ability (body image), language and culture, age, and national origin. In later chapters, the social identities of individuals will be discussed further. However, the importance of this topic for early childhood educators can be summarized in the following statement: The preschool class of 2020 is the first time that the student population is not majority White (Krogstad, 2019). This means that as a nation we have crossed the "majority-minority threshold" and will continue to engage in social environments, including schools, that are increasingly racially and ethnically diverse.

The diversity of the student population is not limited to only race, however. Each individual person has multiple identities, and the intersection of these different identities helps create a lens to view the world. The concept of intersectionality was made popular by law professor Kimberlee Crenshaw in 1989. In an article, Crenshaw describes the complex identities individuals juggle throughout their lives; these identities often overlap with privilege, power, and oppression (Coleman, 2019). Failing to acknowledge the complexity of identities or the intersection of multiple identities within oneself or students "is failing to acknowledge reality" (Coleman, 2019, para. 11).

> **REFLECTION**
>
> Refer back to the Preface, where the theories regarding identity are described. How is the concept of intersectionality supported or not supported by the theories introduced?

Diversity

Diversity has been defined in research and various fields throughout the years. One set of researchers, in the field of science, define diversity as the differences that we see in the world and think about and the different ways to try to solve problems. In addition, diversity is embedded in the analogies we use, the life experiences we have, and everything that makes us who we are as individuals (Swartz et al., 2019). Although this definition is used in other fields, another way to describe diversity in simpler terms is as "all characteristics and experiences that define each of us as individuals" (U.S. Department of Commerce, 2001). Finally, Queensborough Community College (2020, para. 4) states that diversity is "more than just acknowledging and/or tolerating difference." Derman-Sparks et al. (2020) explains that as early childhood educators, we must intentionally use practices to help "children feel and behave respectfully, warmly, and confidently with people who are different from themselves" (p. 16).

In early childhood, diversity is centered in antibias education (ABE), which was discussed in the Preface. As a reminder, ABE is an approach to early childhood education that sets forth values-based principles and methodology in support of respecting and embracing differences and acting against bias and unfairness.

Equity

What is equity in the context of early childhood education? Clark (2019) explains that equity is "the quality of being fair and impartial" (para. 4). Equity is *not* the picture of children trying to look over a fence that is often portrayed when discussing equity (see Figure 1.1).

Why? To explain, Paul Kuttner (2015), a writer at Cultural Organizing, wrote:

> The problem with the graphic has to do with where the initial inequity is located. In the graphic, some people need more support to see over the fence because they are shorter, an issue inherent to the people themselves. That's fine if we are talking about height, but if this is supposed to be a metaphor for other inequities, it becomes problematic. (para. 3)

Essentially, adding boxes, an arguably easy task, does not speak to the structural and institutional barriers individuals face based on historical context that are not an "easy fix."

Furthermore, Aasha M. Abdill (2016), an independent evaluation and strategy consultant in Washington, DC, shared the following on LinkedIn (abridged) regarding a similar figure as illustrated in Figure 1.1:

> While I very much appreciated the intended purpose of the image—distinguishing equity from equality—the first time I saw it, I could not click the "like" button. Something about the image bugged me....

As each LinkedIn colleague liked, shared and commented in its favor, I felt an irrational exasperation. I am not easily vexed so this was a clear problem that I knew I needed to address.

I stared at the image. It "stared" back at me. I frowned. I sighed. I furrowed my brow. I walked away. And, then it hit me. My voice in my head screamed with a mixture of indignation and relief, "That's why I can't stand you!"

Diversity, Equity, Inclusion, Access, and Belonging 7

Figure 1.1. Equality versus equity. (Adapted from Interaction Institute for Social Change/Artist: Angus Maguire. Licensed under Creative Commons at https://creativecommons.org/licenses/by-sa/4.0/.)

Do you know why? If you don't, it's understandable because it exemplifies the insidiousness of implicit bias. So, I will not keep you entrapped for a second longer. Instead, I will ask you one question.

In the picture, why are the three individuals so observably different in capability (physical height and age)?

Social equity is imperative because structural inequality exists; that is, you can predict the outcomes of individuals based on social characteristics that should not have any direct correlation to the outcome. Why then, is it possible to predict? Because, social inequality is perpetuated by institutional and individual discrimination. So, to address social inequities, the boxes appearing in the second frame are necessarily doled out **unequally** so that **equity** can be achieved.

The problem with the picture is in its implicit bias that many do not see. If we believe, fundamentally, that all people regardless of race, class or creed are comparably able, there should be little difference between the individuals in this picture. What should be drawn as dissimilar are not the individuals but rather the bottom boxes they are standing on in the first frame.

While I fully appreciate the intended purpose of the image, its point regrettably rests upon a deeply ingrained belief of the inherent inequality

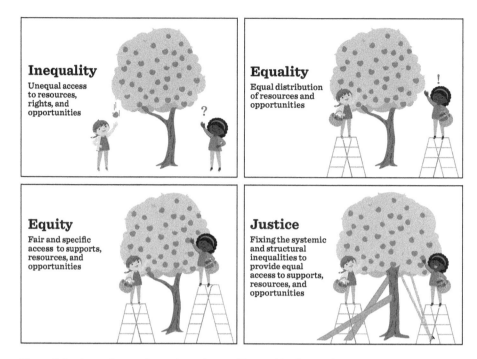

Figure 1.2. Inequality, equality, equity, and justice. (*Source:* Maeda, 2019.)

of people. And, despite the sincere explicit intention for increasing understanding, empathy, and justice for redressing social inequities, the picture's sentiment implicitly reinforces the idea that minorities (or those otherwise unprivileged) have inferior abilities. (paras. 2–9)

What is a good picture or graphic to use when discussing equity with adults? The picture in Figure 1.2 displays inequality, equality, equity, and justice through the use of an apple tree, a couple of ladders, some 2-by-4s, and rope.

> **REFLECTION**
>
> Look at the four pictures in Figure 1.2. Discuss or reflect on how this figure truly shows the definition of equity (and justice).
>
> ANSWER
>
> Look at equity and justice. What is needed on both sides for justice? Work and support are needed on both sides for justice, in addition to fixing the root cause rather than just getting a higher ladder.

CASE STUDY: PROGRAM APPLES

During one of our first meetings with the Program Apples staff, the apple tree graphic shown in Figure 1.2 was displayed on the screen. We then asked the staff members to freewrite for 1 minute on what they observed in the graphic. At the end of the 1-minute (silent) freewriting session, we asked the staff to share what they wrote. Below are some of their reflections:

- "I have seen the first two [top] before, but the bottom two are interesting. This means we have to do work on both sides."

- "Justice is more than just helping the oppressed. It is the powerful doing work also."

- "We need to revisit this often. This is powerful that we need support on both sides of the structure—the structure or structural racism in our country."

- "I don't understand what it is showing us. Why is this the graphic we are discussing now?"

This handful of reflections shows the differences in responses we discussed and continued to discuss throughout the entire process of growth and learning. From the individuals who began to see the structural and institutional isms affecting their learning environments to the staff members who questioned why this was something to discuss, it displays the areas of growth and different places each person was starting from regarding their own process.

In response to these comments, we, the coaches, restated, identified, and previewed concepts that would support the insights of or provide more insights to each participant so that they felt they were in a brave space to share their thoughts and reflections. (*Note:* No one is ever called out or pressured to share because we all engage and learn in our own unique ways.)

Although the apple tree graphic is excellent to discuss with adults, it is not necessarily developmentally appropriate for young children. However, an excellent activity to explain what equity is to early childhood students is known as the "Band-Aid" activity. The activity was originally described by Tumblr user aloneindarknes7. This user outlined their approach to the concept of equality versus equity through a developmentally appropriate activity. So, as you are reading this, think about it in the sense of a young, developing brain (not a developed adult brain with many experiences and a whole lifetime of adventures). (If you are completing this activity with your students, please make sure to have clear Band-Aids or Band-Aids that represent all skin tones.)

In aloneindarknes7's own words:

> This is something that I teach my students during the first week of school and they understand it. I have each student pretend they got hurt and need a band-aid. Children love band-aids. I ask the first one where they are hurt. If he says his finger, I put the band-aid on his finger. Then I ask the second one where they are hurt. No matter what that child says, I put the band-aid on their finger exactly like the first child. I keep doing that through the whole class. No matter where they say their pretend injury is, I do the same thing I did with the first one.

After they all have band-aids in the same spot, I ask if that actually helped any of them other than the first child. I say, "Well, I helped all of you the same! You have one band-aid!" And they'll try to get me to understand that they were hurt somewhere else. I act like I'm just now understanding it. Then I explain, "there might be moments this year where some of you get different things because you need them differently, just like you needed a band-aid in a different spot." If at any time any of my students ask why one student has a different assignment, or gets taken out of the class for a subject, or gets another teacher to come in and help them throughout the year, I remind my students of the band-aids they got at the start of the school year and they stop complaining.

This activity does a great job at teaching equity to children and the principle of giving each child what they need; it also provides an avenue for educators to reflect on teaching practices that often use a "one-size-fits-all" approach. *Note:* We suggest using clear Band-Aids for this activity.

Inclusion

What is inclusion in the context of early childhood education? Simply, it is the absence of exclusion. McManis (2021) describes inclusion as "accepting, understanding, and attending to student differences and diversity, which can include physical, cognitive, academic, social, and emotional" (para. 4). A question we often ask when working with groups of professionals centered on the concept of inclusion is: **Who/what group are you willing to exclude? If we do not include, we inevitably exclude.**

Although inclusion is often focused on the field of special education or students with disabilities/exceptionalities, it is also important to acknowledge other contexts of inclusion. Essentially, inclusion is assuming heterogenous normativity, or the assumption that everything is compared to the socially accepted "normal." For example, a common "it is normal" concept is to have stairs in buildings for people who are ambulatory; however, when ramps are added, it is considered "inclusive." Another "normal" that is often portrayed in classrooms, through language and books, is the concept of what a family looks like: a mom, dad, and children. The diversity of homosexual families, single-adult families, foster or adoptive families, multigenerational families, and so forth is not presented or included and thus provides a message (through silence) about what is normal and what is abnormal.

Now that we may have started you on a trajectory of thinking about inclusion in a critical way, reflect on the following quote by Reinking (2020): "Inclusion means the structure is made for everyone. Transformation is actually what we need to be doing. Don't focus on inclusion into a broken system but transform the broken system so that inclusion is inevitable."

> **REFLECTION**
>
> Read the quote by Reinking (2020) again. What is your initial reaction to the quote in terms of transformation? (Remember, the history of school was that formal education was built for White, wealthy Christians.)

True transformation in early childhood learning environments focuses on critically examining the hidden curriculum embedded into the classroom. Are there metaphorical windows, mirrors, and sliding glass doors in the learning environment, curriculum, and language?

You may be asking yourself, "What do you mean by metaphorical windows, mirrors, and sliding glass doors?" These are concepts coined in the literacy field, but they come into play when discussing hidden curriculum or curriculum that has historically been centered in ableism, eurocentrism, and heteronormative practices.

Metaphorical windows mean that children in your classroom can "see" into the lives of people who do not share their identity. The diversity of the community, country, and often world is presented in the classroom through a "window." The important thing to be aware of is that when embedding windows there should be no "token" or stereotypical images or assumptions made by the artifacts or media (books, music, or posters) in the learning environment. For example, we often enter early childhood classrooms that have many misconceptions about Mexico, such as all Mexican food is spicy, Halloween and the Day of the Dead are the same thing, burritos and fajitas are Mexican cuisine (they are actually just Americanized food often served at Mexican restaurants in the United States), and all Mexicans speak Spanish (currently, 92% of Mexicans speak Spanish, but not all Mexican speakers speak Spanish or are as fluent in Spanish as in their indigenous languages [Zyzdryn, 2020]). Embedding the concept of windows, in this example, would be to research and ensure that stereotypes or misconceptions are not taught through a westernized view of people who live in Mexico.

Metaphorical mirrors mean that children can see themselves represented in the classroom or learning environment. As is often said, representation matters. An easy way to embed mirrors of children into the classroom is through a family flag activity that is implemented throughout the school year. The case study used throughout this book provides a fantastic example of creating a yearlong family flag activity, which is described in a future chapter. However, a short description of the activity is that it encourages families to make a "family flag" (poster board or 8 × 11 paper) of items that are important to them as a family. It could include pictures of family members, words or pictures of activities the family enjoys together, or even things that are specific to the child in the classroom such as their favorite color or food. Creating these flags, posting the flags around the room, and discussing the flags (and ultimately the culture of the family) throughout the year bring families into the classroom on a daily basis.

Metaphorical sliding glass doors can easily be explained as embedding identities into your classroom so deeply that the children feel immersed. One example we often use during workshops is one that we experienced while working with Program Apples.

CASE STUDY: PROGRAM APPLES

The concept of metaphorical sliding glass doors is when you completely take over an environment so that you feel as if you are truly in the environment. In Program Apples, one classroom did this seamlessly. The teachers in the classroom chose several diverse books regarding hair, barbershops, and hair salons. Then, over the course of 1 week, they completely redid their classroom to emulate a hair salon/barbershop that may be seen in various communities. There were pictures of racially diverse children with different hairstyles including braids and natural hairstyles posted in the dramatic play area. Images that can be found in many barbershops showing various haircuts were displayed throughout the classroom. There were various real and pretend hairstyling tools such as blow-dryers and flat irons (with the cords removed), spray bottles, combs, and empty containers of hair products for the children to use on the dolls. In the block center, the children made blueprints of what their hair salon/barbershop building would look like and then used blocks to construct a model of the building. In the writing center, the students were able to design signs for their barbershop/hair salon. The teachers incorporated literacy and math by having the students write out the services and price of the service (haircut/style). By the end of the week, when the transformation was complete, the students were fully embedded into a simulated hair salon/barbershop.

In an early childhood classroom or learning environment, providing metaphorical sliding glass doors could be transforming the classroom into a salon/barbershop, having books about people going to the hair salon/barbershop, and fully embedding the concepts of hair, cutting hair, and the various meanings of hair for groups of people.

> **REFLECTION**
>
> What are ways you have created metaphorical mirrors, windows, and sliding glass doors in your early childhood learning environment?

CASE STUDY: PROGRAM APPLES

Program Apples reflected on the windows, mirrors, and sliding glass doors in their learning environments, specifically focused on the books in the classroom. Through this reflection process, Program Apples decided to buy new books to create more windows and mirrors, with the hope of building a foundation for creating sliding glass doors.

Through collective research and discussion, the team of educators decided to choose books that were located on the Here Wee Read website, specifically, the 2020 Ultimate List of Diverse Children's Books, with titles such as *Always Jackie*, *Bread for Words*, and *Hosea Plays On*.

Access

What are access and accessibility in the context of early childhood education? Ensuring access means that barriers to opportunities are eliminated, pathways for families and students to fully engage in the learning environment are fully provided, and all students/families are appreciated for their complete selves. Are there accessible parking spaces for families? Are the marketing and communication materials that promote events accessible for all? Are the toys in the classroom accessible for all children? Are the activities the school embeds into the daily schedule accessible for all children, regardless of their ability or "dis"-ability? Overall, are there accommodations that create a least restrictive environment?

When discussing accommodations, it is important that we all have the same definition of accommodation. An accommodation is a physical and/or environmental change to the learning environment that creates a space for all students to demonstrate what they know. For example, an accommodation for students who are English language learners would be to assess them in their home language (Special Education Resource, 2020). Accommodations are integral to access.

In an early childhood environment, access looks, feels, and sounds like purposeful play full of learning as well as building a sense of community. Access also means children and families have access to all learning within the environment. How does this affect children? I (Thigpen) once lived in an area that prevented me from getting a library card from the public library due to the address of my home. By not being able to access the library, I did not have access to books, media, and other services libraries provide. I was not provided the access to, arguably, a right I have as a member of a community.

Lack of access can be a lack of access to resources, such as described above, but it can also include lack of access to the categories at the base of Maslow's Hierarchy of Needs (see Figure 1.3), specifically, physiological and safety needs, such as a lack of access to affordable high-quality childcare, fresh produce (food desert), and affordable and safe housing, as well as a lack of access to a community with low crime rates.

> **REFLECTION**
>
> What does access or lack of access look like, sound like, and feel like in your early learning environment?

Belonging

What is belonging in the context of early childhood education? Belonging is the undeniable feeling of being welcomed. However, it is important to remember that everyone feels welcomed in their own way. We cannot live

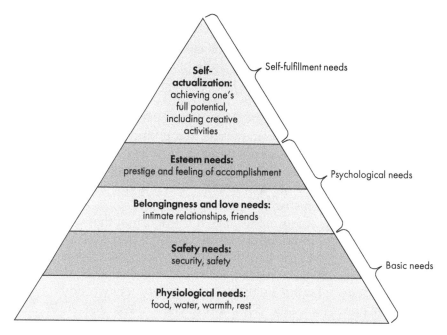

Figure 1.3. Maslow's Hierarchy of Needs. (Adapted from Maslow, A. H. [1943]. A theory of human motivation. *Psychological Review, 50*[4], 370–396. https://doi.org/10.1037/h0054346. In the public domain.)

by the "Golden Rule" (I centered) of treating others the way we want to be treated, but rather, we should live by the "Platinum Rule" (you centered) of treating others the way they want to be treated. When creating an environment where everyone feels undeniably welcomed, we must ensure that we know what each person needs to feel welcomed (and safe).

How do families want to be welcomed? How do children feel safe?

An anecdote I (Reinking) often share in workshops focuses on the concept of a "calm down corner." In many early childhood learning environments, the calm down corner is full of soft things, such as beanbags, stuffed animals, soft fidgets, and big pillows. Classrooms that are arranged in this way are fulfilling the Golden Rule of intrinsically agreed upon norms of what it means to feel comforted and calm. However, I do not feel comforted and calm in soft areas. For me to feel safe, welcomed, and calm, I need hard chairs to push on and feel my body against, I like to have fidgets that are hard plastic, and I crave other angular items to rub my hands on. Therefore, when a classroom includes a calming area with soft objects, the Golden Rule is being implemented. Conversely, by providing many different calming spaces around the classroom (student choice), the Platinum Rule is being implemented, and therefore, a sense of belonging is being embraced.

One way to continually focus on the concept of belonging is to reflect on the 4 Crucial Cs created by Betty Lou Bettner and Amy Lew (1990). The 4 Crucial Cs are connect, courage, capable, and count. Betty Lou Bettner, a

Diversity, Equity, Inclusion, Access, and Belonging 15

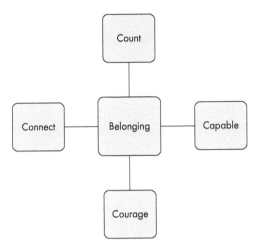

Figure 1.4. The Four Crucial Cs of belonging.

family therapist and social worker, identified these 4 Crucial Cs that work together to help us feel a sense of significance and belonging in a constructive healthy way. Children, as well as adults, are constantly seeking ways to feel that they connect to others, that they are capable, that they count (are valued), and that they have courage. By focusing on the 4 Crucial Cs for each individual, a true sense of belonging is created (see Figure 1.4).

Examples of the 4 Crucial Cs, in the context of early childhood, include the following:

- *Count:* When a child is absent, they are missed, and you let them know it. When they come back to school, they are welcomed. In addition, implementing classroom jobs is a great way for children to feel as if they count as part of the community. Another way an entire school community can create a sense of counting is to welcome children, regardless of what time they show up, with a smile and a positive "Good morning" or "Good afternoon" greeting. When children are greeted with questions such as "Where have you been?" or "Why are you always late?" it decreases their sense of belonging.

- *Capable:* A child feels capable when the adults in their lives have provided them with the skills, knowledge, and foundation to complete what they are asked to complete. For example, children are provided the scaffolded guidance to complete a lacing activity or cutting with scissors on a line. The classroom consists of appropriately sized shelving and furniture that allows the student to independently move throughout the room.

- *Courage:* This is supported by the notion of "If I [the child] fail, I know I will learn." Essentially, children feel supported, and therefore courageous, to try, not succeed, and learn with the concept of "failing forward," which is learning something from a failure to continue to gain knowledge and skills. Teachers use language to motivate children to try new or more complex activities, and children are encouraged to reflect on why they were not successful to learn for next time. Most importantly, children are given the opportunity to try the activity again with the newly learned knowledge and skills.

- *Connect:* Teachers can create a sense of connection through welcoming activities where children learn each other's names or complete collaborative problem-solving activities such as answering the question of the day. Teachers encourage peer interaction by allowing multiple children to "learn through play" in the various centers in the classroom.

> **REFLECTION**
>
> How do the concepts of diversity, equity, inclusion, access, and belonging intersect with the 4 Crucial Cs? How is the concept of belonging supported in your learning environment?

The concept of belonging is not only important (and a newer piece of the diversity, equity, inclusion, access, and belonging [DEIAB] concept) but also assists all individuals as they traverse their path up the mountainside. Arguably, critics of DEIAB say that the work should be changed to belonging, justice, and dignity (BJD) (Davis, 2021). Why do they suggest this change from DEIAB to BJD?

- Belonging is one's physical, emotional, and psychological safety—the indescribable feeling of being welcome.
- Dignity is one of the most universal concepts to describe the sacred nature of each individual's personhood.
- Justice is the repairing and restoring of individuals.

As is evident from the definitions, BJD focuses more on individual identities and repairing a history of oppression and power dynamics.

> **REFLECTION**
>
> After reading these definitions, go back to Figure 1.2 showing the tree that was used as the updated version of understanding equity. How does the figure provide a place for reflection and growth in all of our learning spaces?

MYTHS OF EQUITY

Finally, stemming from many of the concepts introduced and discussed in this chapter, it is important to ground our thinking in a concept known as the "Myths of Equity."

What are the Myths of Equity? They are a list of myths that are often accepted when discussing equity-focused work, specifically in the field of early childhood. Therefore, we are going to take time to address each of these myths.

Myth #1: Children in early childhood are too young to learn about equity. As stated earlier, children as young as 6 months are aware of race and gender differences and are beginning to form ideas about diversity. These same children are growing older and experiencing their own power and privilege, or lack of power and privilege, based on their identities. Although some may question if teaching about equity is developmentally appropriate, the truth is that children are already learning about DEIAB through life experiences and their understanding of fairness. It is important that we create schools and organizations that are a place where our students can be their authentic selves without the punishment that society has placed on historically marginalized identities.

Myth #2: It is fine to just keep things like they are. The fear of the unknown can stop us from questioning practices that we have always done. If we are truly going to transform environments for all, we cannot continue to use the same policies and expectations that we have always used because, frankly, they are built on exclusionary practices and mindsets.

Myth #3: This is just more work for teachers. Change takes time and intentionality. DEIAB work is not just another task for teachers to complete once a year. Building equitable learning environments requires individuals to constantly question, reflect, analyze, and implement transformative practices. Through this process, teachers will be able to learn how their own socialization and privilege or oppression have influenced the hidden curriculum in their classrooms. Yes, it does require effort, but these reflective practices are part of the learning and growing journey.

Myth #4: "I don't see color." The world that we live in is becoming more and more diverse. In fact, as stated in the Preface, the preschool class of 2020 is the first class to have a majority of students who identify racially as Asian, Black, Latinx, Native American, biracial, or multiracial. Therefore, when teachers choose not to see the whole child, including all of the child's identities, educators are using privilege, consciously or unconsciously, to decide who is seen (represented) in the classroom. By stating, "I don't see color," the message is, "I do not see all of you." Furthermore, when "I don't see color" is stated, the intentional representation of all students in the curriculum is also often absent. As Bishop (1990) explained, "When children cannot find themselves in books, or when they see themselves presented only as laughable stereotypes, they learn a powerful lesson about how much they are undervalued in the society in which they are part" (p. 5).

Although you may not personally believe in the myths listed, they are documented and prevalent in education. Therefore, take time to truly reflect on your reactions to the five myths described. If needed, take some of the information regarding definitions into consideration when reflecting as part of your overall journey of growth, learning, and discovery.

2

Purposeful Language to Coach and Lead

"Leadership is not bullying and leadership is not aggression. Leadership is the expectation that you can use your voice for good. That you can make the world a better place."

—Sheryl Sandberg

Language is powerful. Language carries meaning, history, and sometimes a punch. The way we use language, both verbal and nonverbal, is important. Therefore, it is important that you, as the coach, lead educators through the processes of learning, reflecting, and transforming with purposeful language because language is a vehicle. It is a vehicle for making decisions, resolving disputes, enacting practices, measuring results, and sharing innovation and creativity. Like any other language, the language of leadership has to be learned, honed, and practiced (Daskal, 2017). It is not an easy process. There will be bumps in the road. But, with continuous reflection and conversations with peers who push you to learn, the language of leadership, specifically in the field of DEIAB, will become a place of uncomfortable comfort rather than fear.

What is purposeful language? In this book, we focus on purposeful language associated with DEIAB, which includes thoughtfully planned actions and words. Throughout this book, you may learn new terms, see the world through a different lens, or reflect on past and future experiences. All of this is part of the planning or premeditated act of thoughtfully using language to call peers, colleagues, and learners into the conversation (calling in) rather than pushing them away (calling out). In this chapter specifically, we continue the learning journey of purposefully using language as a way to include and transform an early childhood environment.

PURPOSEFUL LANGUAGE AROUND IDENTITY

We all have different identities, and our identities make us unique and different. A great place to start the conversation around identity, after grounding yourself in the definitions of DEIAB, is by using the Social Identity Wheel.

Through the process of completing and engaging with the Social Identity Wheel, independently and with the wider group, you will refresh your learning regarding the theories introduced in the Preface. Remember that we are grouped, based on our identities, into in-groups and out-groups. We are grouped by social identities primarily based on social, physical, and mental attributes. Some of the identities are visible, such as race, and some are less visible, such as sexual orientation or hidden (dis)abilities. Remember, as humans, we have a tendency to want to organize or categorize people by their identities, which involves the innate human process of using associations.

The Social Identity Wheel is usually an activity completed in the first or second meeting or workshop; however, for the context of purposeful language, we will introduce it here. The Social Identity Wheel identifies the following social groups: race, ethnicity, gender, sex, sexual orientation, religion, socioeconomic status, physical/emotional/developmental (dis)ability (body image), language and culture, age, and national origin. It provides the impetus for in-depth reflection of our social identities and invites individuals to determine their self-identified group(s).

REFLECTION

Take a moment to write down your identities based on the Social Identity Wheel provided in Figure 2.1. After exploring and identifying your identities, reflect on the following questions, which correspond to the identities listed in the middle of the wheel:

- Which identities do you think about most often in your daily life (i.e., those most salient to you)?
- Which do you think about least often?
- Which of your identities do you think are most salient to students (i.e., you would like to learn more about)?
- Which of your identities do you think have the strongest effect on how you perceive yourself?
- Which identities have the greatest effect on how others perceive you? (Which put you in a dominant position, and which put you in a subordinate position?)

Finally, take time to reflect on your own students or coachees: What do you know (not assume) about your students' or coachees' identities? How do you know that? How are your identities and your students' or coachees' identities similar? How are they different?

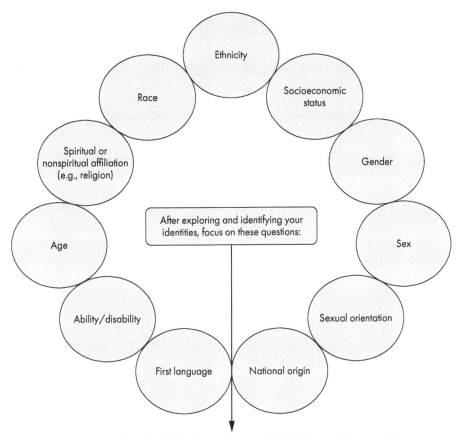

1. *Which identities do you think about the most in your daily life (it's most salient to you)?*
2. *Which do you think about the least?*
3. *Which of your identities do you think is most salient to students?*
4. *Which of your identities do you think have had the greatest effect on your life?*
5. *Which identities put you in a dominant position, and which put you in a subordinate position?*

Figure 2.1. Social Identity Wheel handout/directions. (*Source:* University of Michigan, n.d.)

When reflecting on the various identities and possible answers, the concept of purposeful language is important. A great resource for language definitions is Diversity, Equity, and Inclusion—Glossary of Equity-Related Terms, Version 3 (2022). However, let's take a deeper dive into each of the identities on the Social Identity Wheel starting at the top left.

What is race? According to Gannon (2016), "Race is a social construct without biological meaning" (para. 2). When discussing race, many topics and purposeful language scenarios can arise. One is the word "Caucasian." Although it is understood that Caucasian describes people from the Caucasus mountains, there is also a deeper meaning. In the book *This Book Is Anti-Racist*, by Tiffany Jewell (2020), the history of the word Caucasian is described as a man using the term to describe "the most beautiful." Therefore, in our workshops, we avoid using the word "Caucasian" because of the historical meaning. We provide the context of the meaning and encourage our participants to use the word "White."

Along those same lines, we avoid using the term "person of color." However, we do use the perceived more inclusive and updated term of BIPOC+, which means Black, Indigenous, and People of Color. We do recognize that both person of color (POC) and BIPOC+ are problematic; therefore, we discuss the problematic parts and state that we choose to use the term BIPOC+ to create socially acceptable inclusive, rather than exclusive, workshops and learning sessions. However, if the group of learners is ready for a deeper discussion around race and color, we discuss the history, the meaning, and the use of different words and terms. So, why are the terms POC and BIPOC problematic? White, just like black and brown, is a color. When stating that someone is a "person of color," it insinuates that white is a not a color and is the norm, whereas every non-White person is abnormal because they are "of a color." Therefore, if we do not use BIPOC+, we generally use the terminology "Black" and "Brown."

As we move around the Social Identity Wheel to ethnicity, it is important to note that ethnicity and race are not synonymous and that both race and ethnicity are social constructs designed by social scientists as a way to categorize people. Neither race nor ethnicity is based in biological science. So, what is ethnicity? Simply, it is a category to identify people who are descended from a shared place, such as German, Irish, Mexican, or African American. However, according to the U.S. Census, ethnicity has two categories: Hispanic/Latino or not Hispanic/Latino. We are hoping that this statement from the U.S. Census causes at least two questions to circle around in your mind around purposeful language.

1. Why list both Hispanic and Latino? According to Cunic (2021), "Hispanic usually refers to people with a background in a Spanish-speaking country, Latino is typically used to identify people who hail from Latin America" (para. 1). Therefore, people who are Hispanic may vary in race or their geographic location. Conversely, Latino refers to the geographic location of Latin America only (Cunic, 2021).

2. Why does ethnicity only have two choices? First, it is important to note that our current U.S. Census defines Hispanic or Latino as "a person of Cuban, Mexican, Puerto Rican, South or Central American, or other Spanish culture or origin regardless of race" (Arroyo, 2020, para. 3). There are only the options of Hispanic/Latino or non-Hispanic/Latino because Hispanic/Latino indicates an ethnic origin in a Spanish-speaking (as compared to English-speaking) country, most of which were historically Spanish colonies. Furthermore, within the ethnic category of Hispanic/Latino, there is racial diversity. Although not explicitly stated in easily accessible research, the ethnicity categories are based in early 1900 social science that looked at who colonized parts of the world, English or Spanish speakers, which thus began the concept of ethnicity.

Next, going clockwise on the Social Identity Wheel, is socioeconomic status (SES). According to Worthy et al. (2020), SES is "an economic and social combined total measure of a person's economic and social position in relation to others, based on income, education, and occupation." However, in everyday language, SES often only refers to the financial identity of an individual. An SES identity, in relation to the Social Identity Wheel, is important because your SES affects the resources to which you do or do not have access. For example, individuals with a higher SES identity have access to healthy unprocessed food, updated school resources, and extracurricular activities. Individuals with a lower SES identity often live in communities that are food deserts, which decreases access to fresh produce; attend schools with dated resources; and have limited spendable funds for extracurricular activities. An important note is that many people are one paycheck away from experiencing poverty or living in the lower socioeconomic class; therefore, adding the language of "temporarily middle class" and similar terms is another piece of purposeful language.

The next three identities on the Social Identity Wheel are gender, sex, and sexual orientation. The simple description for these three concepts, which are often new concepts to groups we work with, is that sex is what is on your birth certificate, gender is how you feel and identify within the context of gender socialization, and sexual orientation is who you are romantically attracted to. Specifically, gender is how you identify on the spectrum of gender from cisgender to transgender. Cisgender is when your personal identity and gender correspond to your birth sex. Transgender is when your personal identity and gender do not correspond to your birth sex. There is a whole spectrum between cis- and transgender. As seen in Figure 2.2, sexual orientation refers to who you are physically and emotionally attracted to. If you need any additional information on these concepts in order to develop your purposeful language, great resources include thesafezoneproject.com, The Trevor Project, GLSEN, or the Gender Unicorn (University of Nebraska Omaha, n.d.) (shown in Figure 2.2).

> **REFLECTION**
>
> As a coach, what discussion questions could you pose regarding the Gender Unicorn? How could you relate this graphic to the work of your program?

Next on the Social Identity Wheel is national origin, which is another term for citizenship. Examples include the United States, Nigeria, Korea, Turkey, Argentina, or France. At times, participants will discuss their genetic origins that they may have learned through genealogical mapping or DNA testing based on ancestry. Other times, participants are unclear of what this term means or do not have a strong personal concept of their national origin identity.

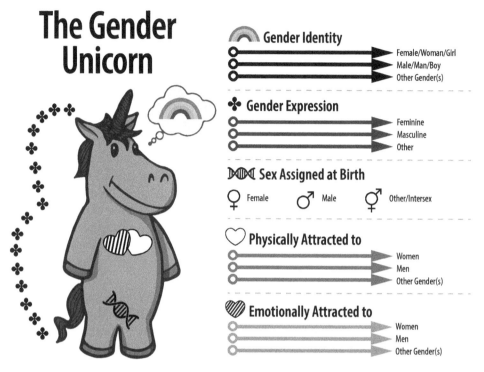

Figure 2.2. The Gender Unicorn (Adapted from Pan, L., & Moore, A. [n.d.] Queer and Trans Spectrum Definitions. University of Nebraska Omaha. https://www.unomaha.edu/student-life/inclusion/gender-and-sexuality-resource-center/lgbtqia-resources/queer-trans-spectrum-definitions.php)

The next identity on the wheel is first language. If we were to update this category, we might add languages spoken or languages used for communication. However, within the constructs of this activity, we purposefully discuss the use of "standard" (i.e., "broadcaster") English, especially in the context of discussing African American Vernacular English (AAVE)/African American English (AAE)/African American Language (AAL), once referred to as Ebonics, is a recognized language with rules. Therefore, students who code switch between "broadcaster" English and AAE are bilingual. Broadcaster English is another way to identify what is often referred to as "standard" English and is easily explained by turning on the news and listening to the speech patterns of new broadcasters. Other languages that our participants often list include English, Mandarin, French, and Spanish.

CASE STUDY: PROGRAM APPLES

When moving around the Social Identity Wheel, we asked the participants (staff) to "judge us by our cover," meaning to go around the Social Identity Wheel and identify our identities. When we reached the "First Language" section, participants stated that the first language for both of us was English, which is somewhat true. However, Thigpen stated, "Yes, I speak English, but I also speak African American Language or Black Language. As educators, it is so important to understand all children have assets to their language. So, when we, or teachers, correct and criticize Black or English Language Learners students' language, especially the language they often use at home, it can create an unsafe environment."

Upon hearing this, one of the participants stated, "I never thought of it like that. I don't correct people who speak slower with a southern accent, but why do I feel the need to correct a student who is speaking, what was it called, AAE?"

Moving clockwise around the Social Identity Wheel, the next identity category is physical, emotional, developmental (dis)ability. When discussing this section of the identity wheel, participants often do not know what to document because of the limited definitions of "ability" and "disability" in wider society. However, this is an all-encompassing identity—brain health (emotional) and physical differences. Furthermore, it is important to note the language of "temporarily able-bodied" and "temporarily disabled." Why use this language? This language refers to the inevitability that most of us will experience a disability at some point in our lives. It could be temporary due to, for example, an accident or longer term. It could occur sooner or later in one's life depending on one's circumstances. Using this language is also a way for disability activists to quickly and effectively bring all of their listeners into one shared community (Hall, 2018).

Age is the next identity on the wheel and is another identity that affects how people relate to or treat each other. Specifically, the age categories for the Social Identity Wheel are child, young adult, middle-age adult, and senior. These categories also have generational connotations such as "baby boomers," "millennials," or "Gen Z." When you read those terms regarding different generations, your brain probably went through the automatic association of common stereotypes connected to the generations listed, such as "boomers are technophobes," "millennials are lazy and poorly prepared," or "Gen Z is too tech dependent." These stereotypes, based on age categories, often affect relationships and interactions.

Religious or spiritual affiliation is the final identity, located at about 10 o'clock on the Social Identity Wheel. Purposeful language around the concept of religion or spiritual affiliation revolves around the discussion of a "higher power" or no higher power. Assuming that everyone is religious, by stating "What is your religious affiliation?" centers religion as the norm. Therefore, reframing the question to ask, "Do you have a religious or spiritual affiliation?" creates a welcoming space for a yes or no answer. If the answer is yes, the conversation then is open for a deeper discussion of categories of religious beliefs such as Hindu, Muslim, Buddhist, Jewish, Christian, or other. If individuals choose to categorize the nonreligious or spiritual aspect of their identity, you may hear categories such as pagan, agnostic, atheist, or secular humanist.

> **REFLECTION**
>
> Think about the Social Identity Wheel activity and the discussion regarding identities. What questions do you have after reading this section? How are you going to find the answers to those questions?

INTERSECTIONALITY

As a reminder, intersectionality is the interconnections among our identities that make us who we are as individuals. Therefore, the privileges we enjoy and the discrimination we face are a product of our unique identities and positioning in society as determined by these social classifiers (Cole, 2019). Our intersectional identities create multi-dichotomous relationships between privilege and oppression. Some of our identities, as shown in Figure 2.3, are seen as privileged or powerful, and other identities are viewed in society as powerless or oppressed.

Our social identities can influence the experiences we have in either positive or negative ways. Some identity groups are subordinated, targeted,

Oppressed	Privileged
Black, Indigenous, and People of Color	White/European
Non-Christian (Agnostic, Atheist, Jewish, Muslim, etc.)	Christian
Non-English Speaking (USA)	English Speaking
Living in Poverty/Working Poor	Wealthy/Middle Class
Undocumented American	American Citizen
Female/Woman	Male/Man
LGBTQIA+	Heterosexual
Transgender	Cisgender
Homeless	Housed
Informally educated ("degreeless")	Formally educated ("degreed")
Mentally/physically diverse	Temporarily mentally/physically able

Figure 2.3. Intersectional Identities. (From Reinking, A., & Thigpen, L. [2021]. *Intersectional Identities*. Reinking Education Consulting, LLC. www.akreinking.com)

or marginalized from a historical and institutional level, and others are dominant, privileged, and afforded agencies that members of subordinate groups lack. In our society, dominant groups or identities are socially valued, and as such, they enjoy social capital or have developed networks of relationships that provide support. Conversely, individuals who identify as members of groups that are socially marginalized are constantly reminded of how they are not valued, respected, or represented because they lack social, political, and/or economic power.

Therefore, when discussing identities, pay close attention to the purposeful language surrounding historically privileged and oppressed groups in society. Have open conversations that lead to learning and discourse that do not imply one is "better" or "worse," but that acknowledge there is historical context to the intersections of our identity.

> **REFLECTION**
>
> What are your positions of privilege and oppression? How might these positions affect your work as an educator?

SUBJECTIVE VERSUS OBJECTIVE LANGUAGE

Finally, purposeful language needs to focus on objectivity, which, according to EnglishXP (2021), is:

> a way of talking about things in a way that does not express opinion, feelings, personal biases etc. . . . [but rather] talking in a way that is measurable, quantifiable and is based on data and scientific fact. It also means not exaggerating or distorting the data. (para. 1)

An example of objective language, in the context of DEIAB, is given by Willingham (2019, para. 1): "A study of nearly 100 million traffic stops from around the country has concluded that, on average, Black drivers are 20% more likely to get pulled over than White drivers." This statement is based on facts that are measurable and without bias or personal feelings associated with the statement.

The opposite of objective language is subjective language, which is a type of language that expresses opinions, feelings, and personal biases. Subjective statements cannot be measured, can lead to conflict with other people, and are purely based on opinions (EnglishXP, 2021). An example of subjective language, in the context of DEIAB, is the following: "Poor people are just plain lazy and never seem to care about their kids' education." This is an opinion and is not based on any facts but, instead, is a common misconception that is touted in society regarding people living in poverty.

When reflecting on objective and subjective purposeful language, it is also important to critically think about words that are often embedded into the educational system. Take, for example, the term "at risk." According to Great Schools Partnership (2013b, para. 1), in educational settings, "at risk" is:

> used to describe students or groups of students who are considered to have a higher probability of failing academically or dropping out of school. The term may be applied to students who face circumstances that could jeopardize their ability to complete school, such as homelessness, incarceration, teenage pregnancy, serious health issues, domestic violence, transiency (as in the case of migrant-worker families), or other conditions, or it may refer to learning disabilities, low test scores, disciplinary problems, grade retentions, or other learning-related factors that could adversely affect the educational performance and attainment of some students. (para. 1)

> **REFLECTION**
>
> Reread the list of what constitutes being "at risk" in many education settings. Which are identities that children are born into or have no control over?

The debate around the term "at risk" revolves around a deficit mindset associated with the term as well as an overgeneralization that stigmatizes students who already are part of multiple oppressed groups in our society. As the Great Schools Partnership (2013b) states, educators "may also fear that such labels may perpetuate the very kinds of societal perceptions, generalizations, and stereotypes that contribute to students being at greater risk of failure or of dropping out in the first place" (para. 6). Furthermore, overgeneralizing a group of students by labeling them does not take into account individual demographics that may be seen as factors of resilience such as familial support, community support systems, or other internalized characteristics.

> **REFLECTION**
>
> Now that you have learned about the problematic term "at risk," what are other terms might you want to reevaluate in your setting?

Overall, the language you use as a leader, coach, or educator in the field of DEIAB needs to be objective, based in facts, and display the vulnerability of your own learning. But every conversation is not going to be easy. Sometimes, conversations will be difficult. In Chapter 3, we discuss how to effectively engage in difficult conversations.

3

Communicating Through Discomfort

"The roots of interpersonal conflict are often an excessive concern for oneself, and an inability to pay attention to the needs of others."
—Mihaly Csikszentmihalyi

The goal of equity-focused education, similar to the goal of antibias education (ABE), is to help children realize their fullest potential by providing opportunities for learning in a variety of individualized ways. **So, why is engaging in equity-focused work often difficult? The difficulty often stems from anxiety and fear of the unknown.**

Discussing, and eventually embedding, equity-focused education is often fraught with emotions, from highs to lows. However, in order to make changes in our own learning journeys, along the multitude of paths toward an equity-focused summit, we must all communicate effectively. As Robinson et al. (2019) indicated:

> Effective communication is about more than just exchanging information. It's about understanding the emotion and intentions behind the information. As well as being able to clearly convey a message, you need to listen in a way that gains the full meaning of what's being said. (para. 2)

Communication is important to transmit and receive knowledge, develop relationships, convey messages, and achieve common goals. It can be verbal, such as words, or nonverbal, such as gestures, facial expressions, or body language. Communication helps people express ideas and feelings and understand thoughts and emotions. Furthermore, effective communication is a key interpersonal skill that also corresponds to the idea of emotional intelligence.

EMOTIONAL INTELLIGENCE

Emotional intelligence is a key factor in diving into conversations about equity-focused education and learning environments. In essence, one's emotional intelligence is the ability to perceive, manage, and regulate emotions. Can you read people's emotions? Can you manage your own emotions? Can you regulate the highs and lows of your emotional reactions to ideas, conversations, and actions?

Reflecting on your own emotional intelligence is one of the first steps in becoming aware of your ability and readiness to discuss equity-focused education with people who have different viewpoints than your own.

How do you know if you have high emotional intelligence? Travis Bradberry (2018) outlined 14 indicators of high emotional intelligence, which you will see can be learned and are highly malleable:

1. You have a robust emotional vocabulary. This means you expand beyond the emotional words of mad, happy, bad, and good. You find a word that provides more meaning for the emotions you are feeling, such as frustrated or jubilant.

2. You are curious about people. This indicator is not dependent on your introverted or extroverted nature, but rather is based on the fact that you truly enjoy learning more about the people around you. This often leads to high empathetic responses.

3. You know your strengths and weaknesses. This is accomplished through honest personal reflection.

4. You are a good judge of character, which means you can "read" people pretty accurately. You are able to understand motivations above and below the surface.

5. You are difficult to offend. This is true because someone with a high emotional intelligence is secure in who they are, has high self-confidence, and is open-minded about the world around them.

6. You let go of mistakes. Building on the concept of failing forward, making mistakes is not a failure but is seen as a place to learn and grow.

7. You do not hold grudges. Grudges breed stress, which breeds negativity. An emotionally intelligent person can let go of a grudge and actually is healthier for it.

8. You neutralize toxic people. Toxic people are exhausting; however, someone who has a high emotional intelligence is able to recognize the toxic negative situation, identify personal emotions, and defuel the anger presented in the chaos of toxicity.

9. You do not seek perfection. Perfection does not exist; therefore, emotionally intelligent people are excited about their achievements and look forward to future accomplishments.

10. You disconnect. Simply put, this is taking regular time off the grid disconnected from e-mail, social media, and other connections that may bring you stress.

11. You limit your caffeine intake because it can cause the release of adrenaline, which reduces our rational thinking.

12. You get enough sleep. Stress, yet again, can be a result of not enough sleep. When sleeping, your body recharges. Therefore, people with high emotional intelligence focus on getting high-quality sleep.

13. You stop negative self-talk in its tracks. Negative self-talk is a natural tendency. However, emotionally intelligent people aim to focus on facts rather than negative thoughts.

14. You will not let anyone limit your joy. You derive your happiness and joy from within, which means that your emotional state is not dependent on the opinions of other people.

> **REFLECTION**
>
> After reading through all 14 indicators of high emotional intelligence, which ones do you currently practice? Which ones could you work on? Make a plan for yourself.

The first step is to be able to reflect on your emotional intelligence as a leader in your program guiding this work. The next step is to focus on kind versus nice communication, as well as potentially sticky spots in communication. These concepts are central when engaging in difficult conversations or purposefully engaging in effective communication.

KIND VERSUS NICE

It is important to understand the difference between being nice and being kind, especially when providing feedback, which at times can lead to difficult conversations.

What is the difference between being kind and being nice? (*Hint:* Our goal is kind.) Table 3.1 details the difference between nice and kind.

Table 3.1. Nice versus kind

Nice	Kind
You are always polite to everyone to ensure that everyone feels good about themselves.	You genuinely care about people and their growth as humans.
Passive, meaning at face value you are nice, but then behind someone's back you are not nice about that person.	You make an active choice to be kind.
You are afraid to speak up in unpleasant, difficult situations and therefore may not share your views or opinions.	You always support people's views and opinions but are open to discussion and growth.
You show off and are competitive, which can be detrimental to relationships.	You are kind and experience kindness, which produces the positive hormone oxytocin that decreases blood pressure. Thus, being kind is generally healthier than being nice.
You try to get everyone to like you, even if it is not your true self. Some people you interact with may not truly know you, your views, or your thoughts.	You are true to yourself and your views and take a stance in a respectful way; you are true to who you are as a professional and/or person.

Why should we focus on kindness when interacting in coaching and supervising relationships? Because kindness is contagious! It also helps reduce anxiety, reduce stress, and form strong bonds. Specifically, it will form bonds and a relationship that will help in guiding growth toward equity-focused learning and implementation. Kindness also has the power to deescalate a conversation.

> **REFLECTION**
>
> Do you lean more toward being nice or being kind? How might being nice or kind affect your relationships and communication with colleagues? How can you utilize the Platinum Rule (treating others how they want to be treated) when working with colleagues who prefer nice over kind?

HINDERING COMMUNICATION

When communicating with another person, regardless of your rapport and relationship, barriers and blocks will inevitably arise. To complicate matters, conversations about equity and diversity have been taboo in most groups for generations. Breaking the cycle of not talking about equity or continuing with the status quo takes courage, which often can lead to tension.

A difficult conversation is defined as a situation in which at least two parties are engaged in communication where there is a difference of opinion or perception of the situation, feelings and emotions are running high, or the consequences are significant (Russell, 2009). Difficult conversations often occur in situations where there is fear, a lack of trust, limited active listening, and a goal of winning. In the context of equity-focused education in early childhood, difficult conversations can occur when individuals do not agree on the need for equity-focused education, people are fearful of the unknown, and individuals are anxious about what equity-focused education means for them and their practice of teaching.

A quote stated during one of our training sessions by an educator accurately summarizes this concept of difficult conversations around the topic of diversity: **"We, as educators, are anxious to lose what we know, but we are also fearful of the unknown. We are grieving the loss of what we know as educators, and we are fearful of the new ways of teaching. That is why we are angry."**

When difficult conversations arise, individuals often lean on two common strategies that stop communication: communication blocks and communication barriers. Although these strategies are different, there are many pieces that overlap. Overall, they both lead to the same outcome—stress, anger, fear, frustration, and sometimes, broken relationships.

Communication Barriers

Communication barriers can create challenges in communicating. One communication barrier is language. Communication barriers can involve a difference in actual language, such as not fluently speaking the same language, or be a language barrier based on varying definitions of words used (essentially, a semantics barrier). For example, if you ask a room of people to define respect, you will get a variety of different answers because each person defines respect based on their own background and experiences. Therefore, if we do not go through the process of defining terms, such as respect, for the context of the work, difficult conversations can arise. Grounding communication in common definitions is essential.

Another concept focused on language as a communication barrier is specific to written language. Assumptions or biases are often made when individuals spell words incorrectly, use grammar that is seen as non-"standard," or use the incorrect version of a word in the context of a sentence (e.g., their, they're, there), as well as when there are generational differences within the context of words. For example, my (Reinking) grandmother, who was born in the 1920s, referred to the couch in her living room as a davenport. My father, who was born in the 1950s, refers to pants as trousers. None of these words are incorrect, but if there is a lack of context based on jargon, miscommunication, and sometimes judgment, can occur.

Furthermore, as a college professor, I (Reinking) often receive e-mails and sometimes papers using what I refer to as "text talk," which is essentially the written language used in text conversations. This is language that usually eliminates vowels, uses grammatically incorrect capitalizations, or represents words through acronyms. For example, the sentence, "Never mind; I'll be right back and talk to you then" would look like this in text talk: "Nvm, ill brb and ttyt."

A third communication barrier is cultural diversity, which is the existence of a variety of cultural or ethnic groups within a society. The diversity of cultures around the world and within a community or school building creates an environment of potential barriers. As Malik (2015, para. 4) stated, "Cultures provide people with ways of thinking—ways of seeing, hearing, and interpreting the world." Cultures determine the meanings of words (refer back to language barriers) and views of the world and can increase misunderstandings. For example, two common sayings in certain cultures are "cut the lights on" meaning turn the light switch on, and "I have to use it," meaning I have to go to the restroom. These sayings could be seen as a deficit in language because there are assumptions being made and/or subject words being omitted. However, as discussed in Chapter 2, there is not one standard way of speaking, but a variety of ways to communicate, all of which have rules, syntax, and recognized usage.

Stella Ting-Toomey, a professor of Human Communication Studies at California State University, Fullerton, described three ways cultural diversity can create a barrier to communication. First is the idea of cognitive constraints, or the frames of reference individuals have depending on their background and culture. Second is the idea of behavior constraints, or the behaviors that are acceptable or not accepted in specific cultures. For example, eye contact and personal space are seen to convey various messages depending on the culture. Last is the idea of emotional constraint, or the differing ways cultures display emotions (Ting-Toomey, 1999).

The fourth communication barrier is based on status differences, which relates to the hierarchy of an organization. In some organizations, the status of an individual is of utmost importance. This would be a high-context culture. In other organizations, the status of an individual does not affect communication because everyone is seen as an equal, from the maintenance worker to the superintendent. This is a low-context culture. Interacting in an environment where status matters and everyone is seen as having a hierarchical place can decrease staff morale and motivation, thus creating a barrier to communication between different "levels" of the hierarchy.

The final communication barrier is physical separation, which has more recently affected collaboration and learning due to restrictions based on the coronavirus disease 2019 (COVID-19) pandemic. For example, having all collaborations and problem-solving meetings held virtually is a physical barrier to communication, often based in Zoom fatigue. Other examples include interior workplace design (e.g., walls), technological problems (e.g., lack of Internet), and noise. Overall, physical barriers can create situations where communication is cut off (phone connection), not heard fully (noisy background), or misunderstood.

> **REFLECTION**
>
> Choose one communication barrier that you have experienced in your practice. How did it make you feel? Did it affect your relationships?

Communication Blocks

Building on the concept of communication barriers, communication blocks also affect communication. There are two definitions for communication blocks. A communication block can be "any remark or attitude on the part of the listener that injures the speaker's self-esteem to the extent that communication is broken off" or "any words, tone of voice, or body language that influence a person sharing a problem," resulting in the end of collaborative communication (Klein, 2013, para. 2).

Simply put, communication blocks are coping strategies when fear and anxiety arise in communication. When a conversation occurs that may induce anxiety or fear, we all have a way to cope. Some people might command, others may give advice, and still others may be sarcastic. Although the intent may not be to stop communication, that is often the result (impact).

There are many communication blocks, but here we have only listed a few that directly relate to experiences or conversations that occur in regard to DEIAB:

1. *Interrogating* includes the action of constantly questioning an individual, which often leads to the person feeling threatened (Gordon Training International, n.d.; Popkin, 2003). An example is when a White person questions a Black person regarding the impact of an event, such as, "Why is asking to touch your hair or saying you speak 'White' racist?" As stated by comedian W. Kamau Bell, "I have a Ph.D. in racism because I experience it every day."

2. *Distracting*, which is also referred to as withdrawing, humoring, or diverting, is the action of appearing disinterested in the person and their feelings (Gordon Training International, n.d.; Popkin, 2003). An example is not truly listening or calling someone too sensitive if they state an experience was uncomfortable and should not be tolerated. A specific example is a sexist joke.

3. *Sarcasm* or *ridiculing* creates a relationship where the receiver (person you are communicating with) is less likely to change because of your focus on the negative (Gordon Training International, n.d.; Popkin, 2003). This is similar to distracting; however, the response is a sarcastic response such as, "Oh, you only like jokes if they objectify men, I bet [laughter]. That for sure will not be tolerated here [with a smile and a slight eye roll]."

4. *Moralizing* is when the words "should," "ought," or "must" are incorporated into the response (Gordon Training International, n.d.; Popkin, 2003). An example of moralizing is stating to someone, "Well, you should just learn more about _____, so you aren't so uncomfortable with discussing it."

5. *Know-it-all* is when a message is sent that you know everything and the other person does not. This often occurs in DEIAB work when individuals have different starting parts to their journey. People can feel unwelcomed if the content and learning are not within their DEIAB zone of proximal development (Popkin, 2003).

6. *Judging* or *criticizing* is also known as disagreeing or blaming. This is a communication block that messages to the receiver negative criticism based on evaluations. It is hard to find someone who innately enjoys being judged. Therefore, this common communication block of judging creates a negative self-concept for the receiver, which often is the result of supervision observations (Gordon Training International, n.d.).

7. *Negative emotional responses* are defined by the perception (impact) of the receiver. Regardless, if the receiver's perception results in an emotional or stress response to the sender, such as yelling, crying, or becoming physically or verbally aggressive, or another type of response, this can then create a block to any further communication. In DEIAB work, this can happen when people are learning new information that is uncomfortable and that triggers a stress response (Reinking, 2019).

8. *Gaslighting* is a tactic in which a person or entity gains power over another by making the person question their reality (Sarkis, 2017). Gaslighting is a strategy used to control a situation or person. Examples include creating situations where revisionist history is stated and supported (Reinking, 2019).

9. *Identity* communication blocks, both verbal and nonverbal, are directly associated with various aspects of one's identity. An example would be if an individual shares their preferred pronouns of they/them but you do not use those pronouns or misgender the individual. This can create an environment of exclusion, damaged professional relationships, or even anger. However, communication should not stop because of an internal fear of misgendering an individual. Be reflective, be aware, and focus on inclusion. If you inadvertently misgender, acknowledge, correct, and move on.

REFLECTION

What communication blocks or barriers do you feel you use when interacting with colleagues? Families? Supervisors? Students?

As a coach to teachers or a teacher to students, how can you help others identify when they are using these communication blocks? How can you process the why behind the communication blocks they use?

ACTIVE LISTENING

Reflecting on and being aware of communication blocks and barriers is one of the first steps in truly embracing and enacting the process of active listening because it involves more than just listening. Active listening includes the six concepts outlined in Figure 3.1: pay attention, withhold judgment, reflect, clarify, summarize, and share. As you may notice, many of the active listening constructs are also part of the overall coaching process of embedding DEIAB into a learning environment. Embedded in the active listening constructs are being self-aware, questioning, and reflection.

How do these aspects of active listening relate to our goal of embedding an equity focus into our learning environments? Table 3.2 provides examples and explanations.

> **REFLECTION**
>
> After reading through Table 3.2, reflect on your areas of strength as a coach and areas that need growth.

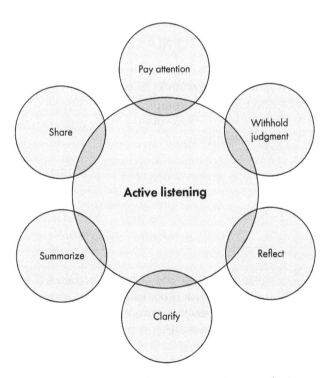

Figure 3.1. Aspects of active listening. (Adapted from Center for Creative Leadership. [2018]. *Use Active Listening Skills When Coaching Others.* https://www.ccl.org/articles/leading-effectively-articles/coaching-others-use-active-listening-skills/)

Table 3.2. Active listening through an equity lens

Active listening strategy	Equity lens
Pay attention	Allow time before responding so as not to cut off the other person mid-sentence or mid-thought. Body language should follow the Platinum Rule (treat others how they would want to be treated). What is body language that makes them comfortable? Eye contact? No eye contact? Sitting? Standing? Multitasking while they are talking to you?
Withhold judgment	Be open to new ideas, perspectives, and possibilities. This includes avoiding interruptions and criticisms. (*Remember:* Just because you do not do it does not mean that it should not be done.)
Reflect	Do not assume you understand the background or experiences of the person you are talking to. Be aware and make sure that you are not stereotyping an individual. Included in reflection is also paraphrasing to mirror the information and emotions of the coachee.
Clarify	Ask questions, especially if something is unclear or ambiguous. Questions could include open-ended, clarifying, or probing questions. The goal is to hear the coachee's voice more than yours. In addition, it is important to clarify any jargon that may not have a shared meaning or be specific to your profession. Or, another option may be to not use jargon but rather use commonly understood language. Jargon may include DAP (developmentally appropriate practices), EI (early intervention), or PT/OT (physical therapy and occupational therapy).
Summarize	Restate concepts or themes discussed during the conversation. Provide next steps and a summary to keep everyone accountable.
Share	Once you have a clear understanding of the conversation, situation, or problem, shift to problem solving through a shared process of communication and brainstorming.

USING COMMUNICATION TO MAKE PROGRESS

One way to make progress through the process of communicating is to develop a common goal. In the context of equity-focused work, a question to ask educators on the path to developing a common goal is: "If we do not want to create and implement equitable learning environments, then who do we want to discriminate against?"

> **REFLECTION**
>
> Stop and think about that question: If we do not want to create and implement equitable learning environments, then who do we want to discriminate against?

Although this is approaching the concept of DEIAB implementation from a more negative mindset, the question leads to internal reflection and a wider discussion. In our experience, the potential discussions stemming from this question are often more difficult in nature, hence the guidance on engaging in difficult conversations.

Although there is not a true answer to the question posed, when engaging in the discussions around the posed question, it is important to help educators understand four concepts: **being uncomfortable is part of the process; intent versus impact; calling in versus calling out; and being okay with nonclosure.**

Being uncomfortable is part of the process of learning, growing, and challenging oneself to change. Often, discussions of diversity and equity challenge our perceived sense of self and our perceived progress and also highlight persistent problems that we have failed to address despite our best intentions. Conversations about diversity and equity force all of us, as individuals and as a group, to acknowledge an unacceptable reality that cannot be fixed with a flick of a switch (Audeliss, n.d.). So, although these conversations may be stress inducing and uncomfortable, embrace the discomfort to further learning and growth.

"Despite our intentions" conversations about diversity and equity are uncomfortable, which leads us to the conversation regarding intent versus impact. Intent versus impact is a concept that has gained increasing traction in the past few years within the DEIAB field; however, it is not a new concept. Intent is associated with the sender's purpose or motivation for communicating in a verbal or nonverbal interaction. A common example is when someone states, "No offence, but. . . ."

Impact is how the receiver perceives the communicated message. How does it make the receiver feel? The receiver may say, "That is really offensive" or simply walk away from the conversation. The impact of communication is what truly matters and is often based on the background and experiences of the receiver.

Essentially, intent does not equal impact. The intent behind an action, statement, or other type of communication is irrelevant. What truly matters is the impact on the person receiving the message. This concept circles back to the idea of engaging in the Platinum Rule, as opposed to the Golden Rule. Be aware of how your words, actions, and practices affect others (focusing on the "you") and disregard the intent of your words, actions, and practices (focusing on the "I").

An example of intent versus impact that is commonly practiced in early childhood learning environments is the representation of children in the classroom. A teacher may be very well intentioned to ensure that children feel represented in the classroom by diversifying artifacts and books. However, if the artifacts and books that include diversity in pictures perpetuate negative mindsets and stereotypes, the intent of the practice is lost because of the negative impact on the child's sense of self in the wider community.

CASE STUDY: PROGRAM APPLES

"What do you mean by intent versus impact?" After hearing this question during one of our first meetings with Program Apples, we (Thigpen and Reinking) shared the following example about the books *Chocolate Me* by Taye Diggs and *Gary* by Leila Rudge.

The book *Chocolate Me* is by a Black author, includes pictures of Black children, and in many circles is viewed as a fantastic book to include in a classroom library by a well-intentioned early childhood teacher. However, when evaluating the words in the book and the messages being sent, the impact is one of negativity.

The first three quarters of the book are about the negative characteristics of the Black main character, with only the last few pages talking about Black joy.

The book *Gary* is about a pigeon named Gary who cannot fly. Similar to *Chocolate Me*, the message is one of deficit. The book discusses all the things Gary misses out on because he cannot fly with his friends. In the world of special education, it arguably mirrors how students who are nonambulatory or are differently abled are left out of many activities their peers participate in. Although the ending discusses the adventures Gary gets to do, it still points out all of the things he does not get to do.

In summary, we told the group that although the intent of the representation (mirrors and windows) is great, the impact of perpetuating a negative view outweighs the teacher's intent.

How can we know the impact of our actions, words, and practices? One way is through the concepts known as "calling in" and "calling out." Calling in is the process of engaging in mutual learning because of a sense of trust and respect for the longevity of a relationship. Essentially, if you are invested in the relationship, you are more likely to call someone in or have someone call you into the conversation regarding diversity and equity-focused practices. Conversations of "calling in" begin with words such as "I'm wondering . . ." or "I'm curious . . ." or "How might someone/your own . . . ." In addition, using "I" statements is another way to call people into the conversation, such as, "I felt _____ when you made that statement/did that action because it perpetuates a negative mindset around women. I would like to engage in a conversation with you on the impact of that statement." These sentence starters provide an opportunity to explore concepts deeper through the exploration of various perspectives, possibilities, and outcomes.

The biggest difference between calling someone in and calling someone out is the focus on reflection versus reaction. When someone is called in, there is mutual reflection, and sometimes, this includes strategies practiced in restorative circles. However, when someone is called out, it is often a reaction to a triggering word, action, or policy. Calling out occurs when a situation needs to be interrupted because the impact of the words, actions, or policies is harmful or unacceptable. It is speaking up when you hear or see something, rather than staying silent. Although calling someone out is uncomfortable, it is necessary to prevent further harm. Conversations that call someone out are also based on "I" statements and the impact of the harmful behavior; however, there is no invitation to speak further about the impact. Some examples of calling out include the following: "Wow, I need you to stop right there" or "I need to push back against that. I disagree. I do not see it that way" or "It sounds like you're making some assumptions that are untrue."

Although calling out and calling in are necessary processes for engaging in difficult conversations, especially around the topic of equity-focused education, it is also okay to end a conversation with nonclosure. Every conversation will not end with a nice bow or a quick answer. Conversations may end with more questions, more room to grow, and more room to reflect independently. So, it is okay to be okay with nonclosure because that is a new starting point for learning, growing, and changing.

Finally, it is essential in this work to build relationships, be aware of our communication blocks and barriers, and actively listen. By actively listening, learning is more likely to occur, growth and change are more likely to be achieved, and staff will feel as if they are truly invested in the programmatic changes occurring to create a more equitable and inclusive learning environment for all. In essence, this chapter emphasizes the necessity of using communication skills to deescalate interpersonal conflict.

II

The Role and Challenges of Coaches and Leaders in Addressing DEIAB Transformation

4

Importance of Coaching and Supervising

"There is no end to education. It is not that you read a book, pass an examination, and finish with education. The whole of life, from the moment you are born to the moment you die, is a process of learning."

—Jiddu Krishnamurti

We are all in a constant state of learning. Even when we fail, we are in a continuous process of learning or, as described by Brené Brown, "failing forward." As already referenced, failing forward is the idea that even if you are not successful, you learned something from your mistakes or failure. That learned experience is then implemented in your next attempt at a goal.

When we are engaging in coaching and supervising, it is important that we see areas of growth as an opportunity to fail forward with the goal of learning and growing. As coaches or supervisors, we can model the concept of failing forward by implementing the adult learning theory, or andragogy.

The adult learning theory was coined by Malcolm Shepherd Knowles as andragogy, which is defined as the art and science of adult learning (Pappas, 2013). The characteristics of adult learning, as developed by Knowles, are built on five assumptions:

1. Self-concept
2. Adult learner experiences
3. Readiness to learn

4. Orientation to learning
5. Motivation to learn

Four principles are also characteristic of adult learning:

1. Adults need to be involved in the planning and evaluation of their instruction (and learning).
2. Experience (including mistakes) provides the basis for the learning activities.
3. Adults are most interested in learning subjects that have immediate relevance and impact to their job and personal life (Pappas, 2013).
4. Adult learning is problem centered rather than content oriented (Kearsley, 2010).

However, to be an excellent coach or supervisor, you must first go through a process of self-reflection (professional and organization). This reflection process will allow you to identify needed areas of growth on a professional and organizational level. Therefore, we have adapted a tool from the Center on Great Teachers and Leaders to use when self-reflecting on your professional identity as well as your organization's identity (Center on Great Teachers and Leaders, 2019) (see Figure 4.1; for full form, see Appendix A).

As you can see in Figure 4.1, there are Y (yes), N (no), N/A (not applicable), Explanation, and Notes sections in the table. Although the Y, N, and N/A sections are used to answer the questions posed in the criteria column, the Explanation column provides an area to explain your original answer (Y, N, or N/A). This explanation is important to document tangible ways this criterion is or is not fulfilled in your professional or organizational work. The Notes section is provided as a way to document actionable next steps to address the criteria. Although these are suggested ways to use this table, please feel free to use the additional columns (Explanation and Notes) to fit your needs.

> **REFLECTION**
>
> After you have completed the self-reflection in Figure 4.1, identify areas of professional growth as well as areas of organizational change. From that list, select one to two areas to intentionally work on.

While reading the sections regarding coaching and supervising, keep these assumptions and principles in mind. Furthermore, coaching and supervising are not one size fits all. As you read and reflect, decide on the role or roles you may take on and flow in and out of in your career. Each role is distinct and important to the overall growth and learning for individuals and the program.

APPENDIX A PROFESSIONAL AND ORGANIZATION CRITERIA CHECKLIST

Attitude and character

Criteria	Y	N	N/A	Explanation	Notes
Does the professional or organization exhibit a strong commitment to the teaching profession?					
Does the professional or organization demonstrate friendly and positive behavior to others?					
Is this professional or organization resilient and flexible?					
Is the professional or organization willing to share knowledge and information with coworkers?					
Does the professional or organization model accountability and ownership?					
Does the professional or organization model continuous learning?					
Does the professional or organization recognize their own limitations?					
Does the professional or organization keep an optimistic attitude about people?					

APPENDIX A *(continued)*

Professional competence and experience

Criteria	Y	N	N/A	Explanation	Notes
Is the professional or organization knowledgeable on the topics of diversity, equity, inclusion, access, and belonging (DEIAB)?					
Does the professional or organization critically reflect on their practices and make adjustments to fit the needs of their students?					
Does the professional or organization collaborate well with colleagues, families, and administrators?					
Does the professional or organization support learning for diverse learners?					
Does the professional or organization have a history of exemplary evaluations?					
Is the professional or organization able to scaffold support over time?					

Figure 4.1. Professional and organization criteria checklist. (Source: Center of Great Teachers and Leaders, 2019.) (Note: A full version of this form is available in Appendix A and to download.)

Figure 4.1. *(continued)*

APPENDIX A *(continued)*

Communication skills					
Criteria	Y	N	N/A	Explanation	Notes
Does the professional or organization have clear communication strategies (written and verbal)?					
Does the professional or organization provide positive and constructive feedback?					
Does the professional or organization use common courtesies (e.g., please, thank you)?					
Does the professional or organization listen more than talk?					

APPENDIX A *(continued)*

Interpersonal skills					
Criteria	Y	N	N/A	Explanation	Notes
Does the professional or organization work well with people who do not share their identity or cultural background?					
Does the professional or organization apologize for mistakes or for treating others without respect?					
Does the professional or organization confront the issue, not the person?					
Does the professional or organization remain curious rather than defensive?					
Does the professional or organization help others view mistakes as learning opportunities?					

(Source: Center of Great Teachers and Leaders, 2019.)

Table 4.1. Coaching goals and when coaching should occur

Coaching	
Goal	Coaching should occur when . . .
• Task oriented • Short term • Develops specific skills for the task • Develops specific performance expectations • Performance driven • Can happen immediately without design (i.e., does not need to be days' or weeks' worth of planning; can happen in the moment, when needed)	• Focusing on specific competencies or skills • Introducing a new system or skill

COACHING

The goals and timing of when coaching should occur are listed in Table 4.1.

> **REFLECTION**
>
> What do you notice in Table 4.1? How might the adult learning theory's assumptions and principles be used in this process?

Coaching is based on a supportive relationship with the goal of providing guidance to develop new skills. Coaches focus on providing feedback, specifically for a desired behavior, and providing guidance on replacement behaviors (what to do instead of the undesired behavior).

When coaching, feedback is vital. There are two types of feedback coaches can provide: positive and constructive. The characteristics of positive and constructive feedback are outlined in Table 4.2.

When providing feedback, the coach should outline the desired behavior, actions, and/or skills that provide the most effective (evidence-based practice) completion of a task. Finally, once the desired behavior is stated or described, the coach provides ideas for replacement behaviors, based on the

Table 4.2. Types of feedback

Types of feedback	
Positive	Constructive
• Details specifics of behaviors or teaching strategies • Explains the impact of the behavior or teaching strategy • Clearly communicates what is effective or successful (based in research) and is outlined in next steps (action plan) • Recognizes positive behavior	• Specifically focuses on the behavior (not the person) • Explains the impact of the behavior or teaching strategy • Remains calm and clear • Selectively chooses only what a person can receive (does not provide too much information, which can be overwhelming) • Watches for nonverbal cues • Listens to the individual's perspective of the behavior and/or situation • Identifies the benefits of improving the behavior (next steps in action plan)

- ☐ Establish a trusting relationship with all employees.
- ☐ Listen more than talk.
- ☐ Speak directly.
- ☐ Value and model continuous learning.
- ☐ Recognize your own limitations.
- ☐ Offer chances to take risks.
- ☐ Remain curious rather than defensive.
- ☐ Model accountability and ownership.
- ☐ Meet others where they are and help them move forward.
- ☐ Keep an optimistic attitude about people.
- ☐ Offer immediate positive recognition.
- ☐ Help others view mistakes as learning opportunities.
- ☐ Help employees work on one skill at a time.
- ☐ Meet individually with employees to identify ways to help them be more effective.
- ☐ Use common courtesies (e.g., please, thank you).
- ☐ Apologize for mistakes or for treating others without respect.
- ☐ Confront the issue, not the person.
- ☐ Demonstrate friendly, positive, and upbeat behaviors to others.

Figure 4.2. Checklist for coaching. (From Reinking, A. [2019]. Coaching Checklist; reprinted by permission.)

desired behavior. Replacement behaviors are new behaviors that replace the ineffective or inappropriate behavior. Often this is written in the form of an individual or programwide action plan, both of which will be introduced.

When reflecting on the process of coaching, it is also important to reflect on how coaching can be implemented with fidelity. A great way to ensure this is with a checklist. This checklist, shown in Figure 4.2, can be completed by the coach but can be even more impactful if it is filled out by the individuals being coached (i.e., the coachee).

> **REFLECTION**
>
> Reflect on the checklist in Figure 4.2. What are areas that might be more difficult for individuals in the role of coach to implement? What might be easiest for people in the role of coach to implement?

Although feedback, desired behavior, and replacement behavior associated with an action plan are the basis for coaching, in the context of this book, coaching specifically focuses on feedback as a way to critically analyze and fully implement equitable practices into a learning environment.

Often, coaching educators to develop learning environment practices through an equity lens is grounded in replacing unintended exclusionary practices or behaviors. Regardless of whether the coach is internal to the program or an external coach, the focus on learning about embedded exclusionary practices (i.e., hidden curriculum or policies and procedures) and developing an action plan to eliminate exclusionary practices is often the first goal.

There are positive aspects of engaging in a coaching model, as well as potential barriers. Overall, coaching improves organizations because of the nonpunitive nature of coaches. Furthermore, if a coach is internal to the program, it has been found that internal support and buy-in is greater. However, regardless of whether a coach is internal or external to the program, when a coach can truly lead educators on a clear path of growth with an equity mindset, inclusive changes are made. Through this process, coaches are able to identify strengths and areas of growth for individuals and the organization overall. From there, coaches can plan ways to engage the areas of strength to address the areas of needed growth.

A coaching model is not always the best model, however, depending on the overarching goals. There are potential barriers to coaching. For example, there are the barriers of time and money. Coaching takes time on the part of the coach as they guide educators through the growth process. It also takes time on the part of the educators who are learning and growing with the guidance of the coach. Furthermore, coaches often come with a monetary price. Depending on the depth and breadth of the work, finding the funds to support the coaching is often a barrier for programs.

Finally, another potential barrier is chemistry, specifically the chemistry or relationship between the coach and the educators. Developing a sense of rapport, especially if the coach is an outside contractor, can be difficult. To develop strong relationships, the coach has to be willing to have direct conversations, must focus on being kind, has to both give and take direct feedback, and must be flexible. As Joy Baldridge (2018) stated in a YouTube video about difficult conversations, we have to be "always flexible and adaptable" in education.

SUPERVISING

In Table 4.3, the goals of supervising, as well as when it is appropriate to use, are outlined.

> **REFLECTION**
>
> What do you notice in Table 4.3 on supervising? How might the adult learning theory's assumptions and principles be used in the supervising process?

Table 4.3. Supervising goals and when supervising should occur

Supervising	
Goal	Supervising should occur . . .
• Task oriented • Evaluation • Monitoring • Oversee a person or group	• To ensure processes and policies are being performed correctly

Supervising occurs between a boss/teacher and an employee/student. In this relationship, the supervisor is the person in power and gives directions to the employee(s) with the possibility of punitive consequences. A supervisor, in contrast to a coach, is the only leader who can give an employee a punitive reprimand for not following through with actions deemed necessary for continued employment. In the context of DEIAB work, the supervisor is the individual who ensures that training moves forward and equitable practices reach children and families.

As with coaching, there are strengths and potential barriers to supervising. Most important, the supervisor has the overall program plan in mind, which, in the case of this book, is building an organization that is truly equity focused. Furthermore, the supervisor knows the educators and has direct and frequent contact with each of them. Therefore, the supervisor can provide guidance to coaches, while also ensuring that the educators are following through with their tasks. The constant and consistent communication with educators is also important because it allows the supervisor to provide feedback and ask questions for clarification and allows employees to reflect on their practices.

Potential barriers of the supervisor role include the perception of mandating a practice of equity focus when not all staff members or educators are in a place of growth and reflection. This mandate perception can cause friction and ultimately impede programmatic change and growth. Furthermore, because educators and supervisors often have close relationships, the friction can result in staff members venting about the DEIAB process to the supervisor who, in turn, may or may not need to take consequential action. The opposite is also the case. Staff may feel that they are not able to freely share their thoughts, assessments, and experiences when a supervisor is leading the equity training due to the possibility of being fired or reprimanded.

> **REFLECTION**
>
> How are the adult learning theory assumptions and principles embedded into the practice of supervising?

SETTING PROFESSIONAL DEVELOPMENT GOALS

Setting professional development goals begins with observation. Observation is needed to know the current reality, as well as to see any future changes or implemented growth. It is important to understand that implementation may be smooth in some areas and rough at other times. A great way to provide feedback on rough and smooth implementation is through a process called "glows and grows." What areas are going smoothly (glowing)? What areas need some assistance to grow? This process helps in the development and continued work of action planning.

Observation Structure

During observation, the coach and supervisor are essentially looking for classroom planning and implementation practices. Slight differences are that coaching is focused on what the *teacher* feels is an area of growth, whereas supervisors often focus on observing staff following *policies or procedures* that are programwide. Examples of what supervisors might observe include cleaning procedures, using developmentally appropriate play-based instruction, or fully engaging with children throughout the day.

After the observation, it is important to schedule a meeting to discuss what was observed and to plan the next steps. A recommended agenda is provided in Figure 4.3.

As you may notice in the agenda, the teacher is always provided the opportunity to discuss what went well and what may not have gone so well during the observation. This provides the coach/supervisor with insight into the teacher's view of their classroom, thoughts on their teaching, and other pertinent information as a guide in advancing the meeting. Does the teacher recognize what they did well? Does the teacher recognize areas that may need to be improved? Understanding the teacher's view of their

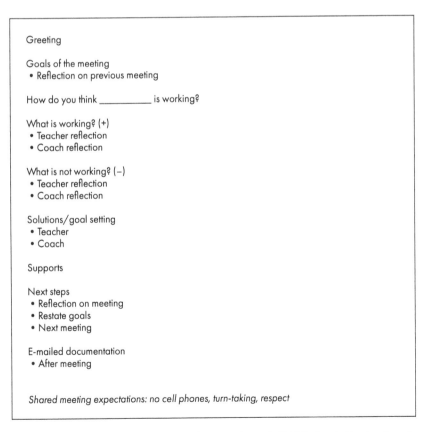

Figure 4.3. Coaching meeting agenda. (From Reinking, A. [2017]. Coach Meeting Agenda Outline; reprinted by permission.)

classroom is a great stepping stone for guiding a reflective, collaborative meeting that focuses on constructive feedback for growth.

During the meeting, it is vital to take notes in order to develop the professional growth goals. The first meeting of the year should include developing the goals. However, in following meetings, discussions on progress toward the goals should be discussed.

As noted in the professional learning goals documentation in Figure 4.4, it is important to not only state the S.M.A.R.T. goal but also outline the resources the coach/supervisor can provide and the resources the teacher will seek out and access. This is a collaborative endeavor to assist in growing professionally.

What is a S.M.A.R.T. goal? S.M.A.R.T. stands for specific, measurable, achievable, relevant, and time-bound goals. What differentiates this goal-setting framework from others is its laser-focused specificity. Specifically, all elements of the S.M.A.R.T. framework work together to create a goal that is carefully planned, clear, and trackable. Whether you are setting personal or professional goals, using the S.M.A.R.T. goal framework can establish a strong foundation for achieving success.

APPENDIX B PROFESSIONAL LEARNING GOALS DOCUMENTATION

Teacher name: _____
Supervisor/teacher coach: _____
Date: _____

Professional goal setting		
Goals	Next steps	Resources/support needed
Goal 1		
Goal 2		
Goal 3		

Goals must be actionable and measurable.

Figure 4.4. Professional learning goals documentation. (*Note:* A blank version of this form is available in Appendix B and to download.)

As part of DEIAB work, developing S.M.A.R.T. goals around the antibias education (ABE) continuum of change will help make progress toward the programwide DEIAB goals. Specifically, the ABE trajectory categories for teachers are resistant, beginner, learner, and mentor.

When discussing observations and goals, it is also important to engage in active communication by restating what you are hearing as the coach from the coachee.

CASE STUDY: PROGRAM APPLES

While coaching one of the staff members through the process of goal setting, the following conversation occurred.

Staff member: "I never feel like I have enough time or energy to do the work of figuring out how to add multicultural books into the classroom. It just seems like a lot of work that is not necessary."

Coach: "What I hear you saying is that you are not sure of the reasoning behind adding in multicultural books to your classroom. I wonder if you could start with choosing one multicultural book and adding it to your classroom and reflecting on how your students interact and talk about the book. Do you think that might be something you could do?"

Staff member: "Yeah, I guess. But I don't know what book to choose."

Coach: "Well, that is something we can work on together. Let us look at a list of multicultural books. I can provide that to you now for you to reflect on before our next meeting. What I would like for you to do is select one or two books from the list. We can talk about these books next time."

Coach (noticing staff member's nonverbal cues: arms crossed, lack of eye contact, and deep breathing): "I want to make sure you are comfortable with this before moving forward. Do you think this is something we can work on together?"

Staff member: "Yes. I mean, I know you are going to tell me they are necessary, but I just don't see the point with all White kids. It just seems like busy work. But I can look at the list and at least try to put one into my classroom."

After this conversation, the staff member and coach were able to design S.M.A.R.T. goals with clear learning action steps for the staff member. Through this process, the staff member had the opportunity to journal, reflect, and discuss questions with the coach as they arose.

> ### REFLECTION
> As you read through the resistant, beginner, learner, and mentor descriptions, identify in which category you think the teacher in the Case Study scenario would fall.

A "resistant" teacher "seems uncomfortable talking about diversity and talks or acts in discriminatory ways" (Derman-Sparks et al., 2015, p. 44). They also have expressed objections to diversity and/or the inclusion of multicultural education or culturally responsive teaching in the classroom or school building. As an example, a teacher in the resistant stage might complain of students or families speaking in their home language at the school (non-English). Another example of a teacher who may be in the resistant stage is a teacher who, when given multicultural materials to put in their classroom, refuses to make the materials available to the children.

A "beginner" teacher "seems unaware of or has little experience with different social identities" (Derman-Sparks et al., 2015, p. 44). A teacher at the beginner stage may make comments focused on denial of differences. For example, they might state, "We are all the same" or "I do not see [color, socioeconomic status, gender, etc.]."

A "learner" teacher "is open to talking and thinking about diversity and is willing to take on new challenges" (Derman-Sparks et al., 2015, p. 44). A teacher who is at the learner stage is open to discussions, seeks out answers, and is willing to learn and implement new ideas into the classroom for the benefit of students and families. Although the learner teacher is open to learning, an educator at this stage does not take an activist stance but rather observes and takes in information. For example, a learning teacher may seek answers on how to best educate students living in poverty but does not change the cost of classroom activities or the expectations of financial participation or have discussions or lessons with students regarding socioeconomics.

Finally, a "mentor" teacher "has expertise and experience" (Derman-Sparks et al., 2015, p. 44) in diversity/multicultural education both professionally and personally. Teachers in this stage are important allies and activists and help schools move forward with transformative practices. Educators in this stage offer suggestions, assist colleagues in their learning stage, and ensure that the school implements culturally responsive teaching strategies in the classroom and throughout the entire school. For example, mentor teachers actively find grants or other monetary donations to assist with the financial burdens many families experience when trying to pay for school supplies and activities.

Associated with the ABE teacher trajectory is the concept known as "zones of comfort." What does this look like for teachers at various levels on the ABE teacher trajectory? It will look quite different depending on where a teacher may be within their comfort zone. Are they in a place of comfort and not interested in change? Are they in a place of fear, which will inevitably hold their learning back through excuse making or a lack of confidence? Are they in a place of learning and ready to acquire new skills? Or, finally, are they at a place of growth and ready to set new goals and strive for new knowledge? Regardless of where a teacher is on the comfort

Importance of Coaching and Supervising 57

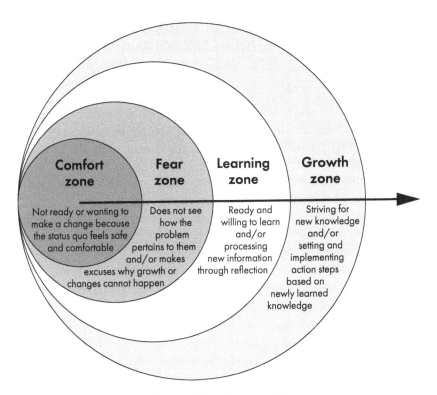

Figure 4.5. The Comfort Zone. (*Source:* Alberts, H., et al., n.d.)

zone scale (see Figure 4.5) and the ABE teacher trajectory, coaches and supervisors can assist in a multitude of ways.

Knowing where a teacher is within the zones of comfort and identifying their place on the ABE trajectory can provide the coach or supervisor with a place to start. This process takes professional knowledge within the context of DEIAB and a relationship with the teacher who is gaining new knowledge to implement and build a plan to guide learning. It is important to note that everyone is unique, and it may take time to know what will work for each individual teacher, while also guiding the wider program change. Regardless of the time it takes to set a goal and reach it, the progress toward the goal is also important to celebrate.

How can S.M.A.R.T. goals and the ABE trajectory be put into action? Here is an example. (It is important to note that the ABE trajectory is not linear, and individuals can embed and flow between the various levels.)

If a teacher you are working with is in the resistant or beginner stage, a S.M.A.R.T. goal for them might be the following: Teacher will read a book focused on DEIAB topics (suggestion: *So You Want to Talk About Race* by Ijeoma Oluo) within 6 months and provide reflection on the concepts learned in reference to an early childhood environment.

An activity for educators who are in the resistant or beginner stage is called the Circle of Trust. This activity begins with writing down the initials of 6–10 individuals they trust who are not family members to see how diverse their friend group is compared to the Social Identity Wheel (discussed in Chapter 2). Through this exercise, it is often found that those who are closest to us share similar identities with us, which is the concept of in-group dynamics introduced in the Preface. Reflecting on this activity, it is important to help teachers understand that because of our in-group and out-group categorizations we have the tendency to have fewer interactions with people who are different from us, which limits our view of society's diverse reality and our intake of outsider perspectives.

> **REFLECTION**
>
> Based on the Circle of Trust activity just discussed, reflect on your Social Identity Wheel and your in-group/out-group interactions.
>
> If a teacher you are working with is in the learner or mentor stage, a S.M.A.R.T. goal may be the following: Teacher will evaluate the hidden curriculum in their classroom using the classroom scan tool. They will then make adjustments based on their score by the end of the school year by using various types of scorecards that are available when searching for "culturally responsive curriculum scorecard" on the Internet. Additional S.M.A.R.T. goals can also be built around researching concepts and providing a professional development to the staff, leading a book study, or summarizing their learning from a podcast, such as the NPR podcast *Code Switch*. As a reminder, the aim of a S.M.A.R.T. goal should be individualized to the staff member to meet their professional needs.
>
> The goal of this chapter is to understand that individualizing the growth of staff members begins with reflection and relationship building, which then leads to developing S.M.A.R.T. goals as part of an action plan. This process takes various amounts of time depending on personal growth journeys. Nonetheless, this process is imperative to the overall programmatic growth in the context of DEIAB.

5

Planning to Start the Work

"Where do I start? How do I build group dynamics?"

As a reminder, as you are diving into this journey of change, learning, and growth, there is no one-size-fits-all model; your organization is unique. Truthful assessment and analysis of your organization's demographics allow for better preparation as you lead others on their journey, as well as progress through your own journey. Just remember, the ultimate end goal is growth—growth toward an inclusive environment that represents all and allows all voices to be heard, seen, and valued.

In this chapter, we discuss the leadership/administrative team that starts and initially leads the DEIAB work.

PLANNING

How do you, as a leader, along with the other leaders in your organization start planning? First, it is important to note that not everyone has to be ready for this change toward an equity-focused, transformative environment. However, with constant support and conversation, most people will develop a deep understanding and fully embrace this practice. Second, it is important to know who on the leadership team will be guiding the work to ensure the DEIAB plan is implemented with fidelity.

Next, breathe. It is easy to feel overwhelmed by the prospect of guiding individuals on a change and growth journey that will, at times, be hard and contentious. It is also important to acknowledge that everyone, including the leader, is on a journey of change, learning, and growth. Once that has been recognized and accepted, it is time to brainstorm and plan the agenda for the lengthy, ongoing, and truly never ceasing process of continual growth.

Who is part of the initial brainstorming? Although there is no correct formula, it is imperative to ensure many voices and views are represented at the leadership decision and planning table, while also pushing back against inviting people as "tokens." A token person is a person who identifies as part of a historically marginalized group who is invited to participate in groups or meetings to "check a box" purely based on their identity. For example, the group that is planning the work should not feel the need to check specific boxes, such as the White man, the gay person, the Black person, the Indigenous person, or the person with a disability.

Once the initial planning group is set, it is time to take inventory of the organization using the Anti-Ism Scale (see Figure 5.1), which can also be found at www.akreinking.com.

ANTI-ISM SCALE

We developed the Anti-Ism Scale after determining that we could not find the "perfect" resource when working with various organizations in our work as coaches. As we work with schools and organizations, many of the tools are specific to one identity, which can potentially lead to exclusionary practices. Therefore, taking many of the tools we already used, such as the Anti-Racism Scale and the work of Banks and McIntosh focusing on multicultural curriculum implementation, we developed the Anti-Ism Scale to be more inclusive of the diversity of identities. The purpose of developing an Anti-Ism Scale, as opposed to an Anti-Racism Scale, was to decenter race and intentionally honor the diversity and intersectionality of identities. Finally, we developed a way to use the scale. Simply stated, you start at the left column. If the answer to all of the bullet points is yes, move on to the next column on the right. As soon as you hit a "no," through deep reflection and honesty, that is the level to start from as an organization.

Note that the asterisks throughout the Anti-Ism Scale refer to historically marginalized (oppressed) identities, many of which can be found in Table 5.1.

Although Table 5.1 outlines historically marginalized identities in the wider society, it is important to note that in the field of early childhood

Anti-Ism (equity-focused) transformation: Continuum for organizational change
Exclusionary monocultural → Cross-cultural → Multicultural → Intercultural and transformative
Deficit thinking → Tolerant → Accepting → Asset thinking → Transformation
Identities (based on the Social Identity Wheel): Race, ethnicity, nationality, sex, gender, sexuality, socioeconomic status, language, ability (dis/ability), age, religion/spirituality

Exclusive (1)	Passive/tolerant (2)	Symbolic/compliant change (3)	Identity/affirming change (4)	Structural/transformative change (5)
Internally and externally intentional or unintentional: • Exclusion of individuals who identify as members of a historically marginalized identity group.* • Segregation of individuals who identify as members of a historically marginalized identity group.* • Publicly enforces the hegemonic (monocultural) institutional prejudices in the form of policies and practices, teachings, and decision making at all levels. • Maintains the dominant group's power and privilege.	Tolerant (recognize, respect, and value differences) of individuals who identify as members of a historically marginalized identity only if they conform to the hegemonic policies, practices, and dispositions. Internally, intentionally or unintentionally limits or excludes individuals who identify as members of a historically marginalized group.* Continues to intentionally or unintentionally maintain hegemonic (monocultural) institutional prejudices in the form of policies and practices, teachings, and decision making at all levels. Uses language such as, "We do not have a problem" or "We will continue with business as usual." *Example:* Stating that since I, as the leader of the organization, do not experience oppression, there is no oppression within our organization. Engages staff in conversations on diversity, equity, and inclusion only when requested or to fulfill funding or other outside requirements and only to the extent that the conversations are within everyone's zone of comfort.	Regardless of the symbolic changes (see below), the culture of the organization does not change due to a fear of making individuals in the dominant (power) groups uncomfortable. Symbolic internal changes: • Officially changes policies and practices to focus on diversity inclusion; however, no real actionable change is observed within the culture of the organization. • Self-identifies as an inclusive environment for all; however, some exclusionary practices are still in place. • Intentional inclusive efforts (e.g., recruitment or bringing more views to the decision table); however, patterns of privilege are still apparent through "token" individuals placed at the table for image more than impact. *Example:* "We have a Black person on the ____ committee."	Develops a wider understanding of power, privilege, and oppression as barriers to intentionally and effectively implementing equity-focused decision making, teaching, policies, and practices. Internally processes and analyzes institutional power, privilege, and oppression. Intentionally identifies as an inclusive, equity-focused organization by developing accountability measures in the active practice of dismantling dominant identity power and privilege. Actively seeks to recruit and include members of historically marginalized identities; however, the power and privilege remain with the dominant identity groups. *Example:* Including individuals from historically oppressed identities "at the table" but not listening to their voices regarding decision making, teaching, practices, and policies. Expanding the definition of diversity to include all oppressed identities.	Commits to the intentional practice of organization restructuring based on analysis of power- and privilege-embedded policies and practices. Restructures all aspects of the organization to ensure individuals from all historically marginalized identity groups fully participate in the organization (i.e., decision making, teaching, policies, and practices). Diversity and equity-focused practices become embedded organizational assets. Commits to impact and actively engage in dismantling oppressive practices within the wider community. *Example:* Creating accountability strategies and rebuilding relationships previously damaged by power, privilege, and oppressive actions.

Figure 5.1. Anti-Ism Scale. (*Historically marginalized [oppressed] identities are listed in Table 5.1.) (From Reinking, A., & Thigpen, L. [2021]. Anti-ISM [Equity-Focused] Transformation: Continuum for Organizational Change. Adapted from Crossroads Ministry, Chicago, IL. Adapted from original concept by Bailey Jackson and Rita Hardiman, and further developed by Andrea Avazian and Ronice Branding; further adapted by Melia LaCour, PSESD.)

Table 5.1. Historically oppressed and historically privileged identities

Historically oppressed	Historically privileged
Black, indigenous, and people of color	White/European
Non-Christian (e.g., agnostic, atheist, Jewish, Muslim)	Christian
Non–English speaking (United States)	English speaking
Living in poverty/working poor	Wealthy/middle class
Undocumented Americans	American citizen
Female/woman	Male/man
LGBTQIA+	Heterosexual
Transgender	Cisgender
Homeless	Housed
Informally educated ("degreeless")	Formally educated ("degreed")
Mentally/physically diverse	Temporarily mentally/physically able

education there are sometimes different relationships between privileged and oppressed groups, specifically in the areas of gender and language. In the field of early childhood education, which is a predominantly female field, male teachers are often oppressed through language of homophobia or assumptions of ill intentions. A common comment is "Why would a man want to teach little children as their career? That is a woman's job." This concept is based on historical aspects of socialized gender roles. In addition, there are many bilingual, dual language, or multilingual early childhood programs or classrooms where a non-English language is valued more than speaking only English.

> **REFLECTION**
>
> As a leadership team, where do you place your organization on the Anti-Ism Scale?

In our experiences as coaches and professional development providers, most leadership teams usually rank their organization at a 2 or 3 on the Anti-Ism Scale. However, when we, as coaches and facilitators, begin to ask how the items in columns 2 or 3 are implemented, the rating begins to fall to a 1 or a 2. Anecdotally, people often state, "I thought we might be lower, but I didn't want us to be at the lowest level. We are not racist, and we are welcoming of all people." Essentially, what we have found is that the initial rating is more of a reflection of who they hope they are as a person versus a realistic evaluation of the overall organization.

Through the process of reviewing the Anti-Ism Scale, the goal is for the team to discuss and identify the diversity (or nondiversity) within the organization from the viewpoint of those at the planning table. Probing questions are a great way to start or continue conversations and open up the environment to true discourse in order to be realistic regarding the current status of the program. Some probing questions to ask the group include the following:

- Who works at your school?
- What are their self-identified identities?
- What race or gender are the employees overall?
- What socioeconomic status do you think they fall into?
- What race or gender are the members of management?
- What patterns of power and privilege do you notice?
- Do the lower paying jobs mainly consist of BIPOC+?
- What language is primarily spoken among staff?
- Are there employees who identify as neurodiverse or require accommodations within the workplace?

These questions, as well as additional questions focused on power and oppression, are pertinent to understanding your organization's realistic starting point for measuring growth on the Anti-Ism Scale. Answering these questions, as well as deeply diving into conversations based on the points in each column of the Anti-Ism Scale, will assist in finding the starting point. The starting point will eventually lead to the creation of a program action plan.

In addition to asking the probing questions, it is important to discuss the Anti-Ism Scale with the goal of transformational change through an equity lens. Below are ways to dive deeper into questions, conversations, and reflections.

Exclusive

The Exclusive rating (1) is the lowest rating on the Anti-Ism scale. The specific aspects of the Exclusive rating are as follows:
Internally and externally intentional or unintentional:

- Exclusion of individuals who identify as members of a historically marginalized identity group
- Segregation of individuals who identify as members of a historically marginalized identity group
- Publicly enforces the hegemonic (monocultural) institutional prejudices in the form of policies and practices, teachings, and decision making at all levels
- Maintains the dominant group's power and privilege

An organization at the Exclusive level continues to enact and follow policies and procedures that do not honor the intersectionality of identities, specifically the identities of historically oppressed groups. For example, such an organization or program might not have accessible entrances or the accessible entrances might not be thoughtfully placed in the building. For example, is the accessible entrance, with a ramp, on the opposite side of the building from the elevator? Is the pathway to the accessible entrance plowed in the winter to decrease slipping? Is the accessible entrance close to the accessible parking provided?

CASE STUDY: PROGRAM APPLES

At the beginning of our work with Program Apples, we engaged with the leadership team to establish a ranking on the Anti-Ism Scale, which was guided by probing questions. We began on the far left of the scale (Exclusive) and moved to the right. When Dr. Reinking asked, "Is your organization here?" most of the group spoke up and said no. However, there was one lone voice that stated, "Yes, I think we are there. One of our buildings is not handicapped accessible. There are small stairs to get in. There is no elevator. Even for people who can walk, sometimes my knees have a hard time with the stairs." The rest of the group began talking about this one building. Statements such as, "We do not own that building, so we cannot make changes" and "We make all the accommodations needed if someone asks" followed. In response to the last statement, I pushed back by asking, "So, it is the responsibility of the historically marginalized person to ask for an accommodation? What if they did not know they had to ask?" There was no clear answer to that question, but it did prompt more discussion.

Finally, a statement by one of the team members summarized this conversation and interaction beautifully. She said, "I would have never thought about that because it does not impact me. That is why this work is so important. It doesn't impact me, so I didn't even think of it as an issue."

At the conclusion of the conversation, it was agreed upon by the leadership team that they were at a Level 3 on the Anti-Ism Scale.

The third bullet point in the Exclusive column uses the term *hegemonic*, which means "leaders, dominance, or great influence." Specifically referring to the statement "publicly enforces the hegemonic (monocultural) institutional prejudices," this includes practices such as idealizing hegemonic masculinity by valuing men, or those who identify as male, because of their assertive, aggressive, dominant, or courageous actions, whereas categorizing the same actions in women, or those who identify as female, as unprofessional, domineering, or "unladylike." Furthermore, hegemonic masculinity within an organization values strength and devalues any form of perceived weakness, usually through the display of emotions (Connell & Messerschmidt, 2005).

Therefore, maintaining dominant group power and privilege would be visible through an environmental scan focusing on who is in leadership positions, who is part of the decision making, and whether there is any identity diversity within the organization. If there is no identity diversity in the organization, at all levels or at any one level, this is a red flag indicating an exclusionary environment.

If an organization self-identifies at this level, the next step as a coach or as the leader of the organization is to focus on the areas that are lacking or need growth. However, it is important to take small steps. If there are too many next steps, it can be overwhelming. For specific ideas, it is helpful to do some research, starting with the following suggestions:

- Exclusion of individuals who identify as part of a historically marginalized identity group
  - *Next step suggestion:* Start small with a book study to learn about historical marginalization in society.

- Segregation of individuals who identify as members of a historically marginalized identity group
  - *Next step suggestion:* Complete a simple environmental scan of the employees and/or students. Are there employees of various races/ethnicities, gender identities, religious identities, and so forth, at all levels of the organization? Are students of various identities in classrooms, and do they participate equally in groups? If not, start to make steps to increase the diversity representation at every level of the organization.

- Publicly enforces the hegemonic (monocultural) institutional prejudices in the form of policies and practices, teachings, and decision making at all levels
  - *Next step suggestion:* Complete a simple policy and practices scan looking for policies that discriminate against gender diversity (make sure to include they/them instead of she/he), racial/ethnic diversity (make sure to follow the CROWN Act or similar acts in states), religious diversity (make sure religious holidays that are not seen as "traditionally Christian" are recognized and acknowledged as days off if needed), and other identity diversity outlined in the Social Identity Wheel. Specific to practices, ensure that inclusive practices are followed through policies, but also in the classroom by acknowledging hidden curriculum and microaggressive language and actions. Although both hidden curriculum and microaggressive language and actions will be discussed later in this book, quick definitions are as follows:

- Hidden curriculum is the unwritten, unofficial, and often unintended lessons, values, and perspectives that students learn in school (Glossary for Educational Reform, 2015).

- Microaggressive language and actions "are subtle behavior—verbal or non-verbal, conscious or unconscious—directed at a member of a marginalized group that has a derogatory, harmful effect" (Hopper, 2019, para. 1).
- Maintains the dominant group's power and privilege
  - *Next step suggestion:* Engage in self-reflection to understand power and privilege in the context of your personal life but also in the context of the wider organization. There is power and privilege in every structure and institution in society, and becoming aware of this fact through reflection, learning, and pushing into uncomfortable conversations is the first step.

> **REFLECTION**
>
> As the leader charged with guiding this work, reflect on your perception of your organization's current ranking. What area do you think the team should focus on changing first? Why?

Passive/Tolerant

The Passive/Tolerant rating (2) includes the following specific aspects:

- Tolerant (recognize, respect, and value differences) of individuals who identify as members of a historically marginalized identity only if they conform to the hegemonic policies, practices, and dispositions
- Internally, intentionally or unintentionally limits or excludes individuals who identify as members of a historically marginalized group
- Continues to intentionally or unintentionally maintain hegemonic (monocultural) institutional prejudices in the form of policies and practices, teachings, and decision making at all levels
- Uses language such as, "We do not have a problem" or "We will continue with business as usual." (*Example:* Stating that since I, as the leader of the organization, do not experience oppression, there is no oppression within our organization.)
- Engages staff in conversations on diversity, equity, and inclusion only when requested or to fulfill funding or other outside requirements and only to the extent that the conversations are within everyone's zone of comfort

An organization at the Passive/Tolerant level continues to enact and follow policies and procedures that do not honor the intersectionality of identities, specifically the identities of historically oppressed groups.

This may include policies that do not allow staff members to hang pictures of their families or talk about their family to their students if they are LGBTQIA+ (lesbian, gay, bisexual, transgender, queer [or questioning], intersex, and asexual [or allies, aromantic, or agender]). Although this did not happen at Program Apples, this exact experience happened at a school I (Reinking) worked at in 2020. A male middle school teacher, who identified as LGBTQIA+, was specifically directed to take down a picture showing his husband because it was a "lifestyle that was not appropriate to flaunt." This is a specific example of a Passive/Tolerant organization.

For many years within the world of diversity and equity, the goal was tolerance. However, with time, research, and wisdom comes the knowledge that tolerance is no longer the ideal goal. Why? Tolerance is defined as showing a willingness to allow the existence of opinions or behavior that one does not necessarily agree with. Even a well-known, equity-focused organization changed their name from Teaching Tolerance to Learning for Justice. As stated in an article by Jalaya Lies Dunn (director of Learning for Justice), the name change reflects "evolving work in the struggle for radical change in education and community" (2021, para. 1). Furthermore, she stated, "We are called as educators, justice advocates, caregivers, and students to reimagine and reclaim our education system so that it is inclusive and just. . . . We must learn, grow, and wield power together" (paras. 8 and 9).

The second point in the Passive/Tolerant column that begins with "Internally, intentionally or unintentionally limits . . ." is also linked to policies and practices. If policies and practices have the impact of exclusionary practices through barriers to groups, such as a financial obligation leading to a barrier, individuals will be excluded from participation in the organization.

If an organization self-identifies at the Passive/Tolerant level, the next steps as a coach or as the leader of the organization, again, should be small but could include the following suggestions:

- Tolerant (recognize, respect, and value differences) of individuals who identify as members of a historically marginalized identity only if they conform to the hegemonic policies, practices, and dispositions

    – *Next step suggestion:* Recognize the meaning of this statement, which is that individuals from a historically marginalized identity must follow the "rules" of the privileged identity. An example of this is a school district led by BIPOC+ individuals that follows the standard practice of overdisciplining BIPOC+ students. If this is the piece needing a next step, it is important to recognize the strengths of valuing differences; however, the next step is similar to the step from the Exclusionary level, specifically, performing an environmental/personnel scan to ensure policies and practices are equity focused for all identities, including historically marginalized populations.

- Internally, intentionally or unintentionally limits or excludes individuals who identify as members of a historically marginalized group
    - *Next step suggestion:* Evaluate the practices that may exclude groups both in the classroom and for personnel. In the classroom, are there financial barriers to access field trips, snack time, and so on? In the classroom, are there barriers for students who have challenging behaviors stemming from trauma, poverty, or racial inequities, and are these students excluded from activities based on these behaviors? The goal of this step is to critically analyze the practices and create a plan to erase or replace the practices.
- Continues to intentionally or unintentionally maintain hegemonic (monocultural) institutional prejudices in the form of policies and practices, teachings, and decision making at all levels
    - *Next step suggestion:* Continuing from the previous level, push to have deeper conversations that challenge thoughts, socialized ideals, and overall practices that continue a monocultural, as compared to multicultural, working and learning environment.
- Uses language such as, "We do not have a problem" or "We will continue with business as usual." (*Example:* Stating that since I, as the leader of the organization, do not experience oppression, there is no oppression within our organization.)
    - *Next step suggestion:* Challenge the thinking of "We do not have a problem" or "We don't need to change" with examples and specific actions to correct the oppressive language/actions within the organization.
- Engages staff in conversations on diversity, equity, and inclusion only when requested or to fulfill funding or other outside requirements and only to the extent that the conversations are within everyone's zone of comfort
    - *Next step suggestion:* As the coach or supervisor, lead discussions, book studies, and wider DEIAB conversations. In addition, push outside of the zones of comfort so that individuals start or continue the learning process regarding themselves and their organization.

REFLECTION

As the leader charged with guiding this work, reflect on your perception of the organization's current ranking. What area do you think the team should focus on changing first? Why?

Symbolic/Compliant Change

The Symbolic/Compliant Change rating (3) includes the following specific aspects:

- Regardless of the symbolic changes (see below), the culture of the organization does not change due to a fear of making individuals in the dominant (power) groups uncomfortable.

- Symbolic internal changes:
  - Officially changes policies and practices to focus on diversity inclusion; however, no real actionable change is observed within the culture of the organization
  - Self-identifies as an inclusive environment for all; however, some exclusionary practices are still in place
  - Intentional inclusive efforts (e.g., recruitment or bringing more views to the decision table); however, patterns of privilege are still apparent through "token" individuals placed at the table for image more than impact. *Example:* "We have a Black person on the ___ committee, so we are inclusive."

This is often one of the toughest levels to reflect on as an organization because changes are seen and can be documented; however, no true change in the actual culture of the organization has occurred. This means that cultural aspects of the organization, such as everyone feeling a sense of belonging, focusing specifically on the Four Crucial Cs (courageous, capable, count, and connect), providing equitable pay, and pushing against hegemonic decision making have not occurred.

If an organization self-identifies at the Symbolic/Compliant Change level, the next steps as a coach or as the leader of the organization, again, should be small steps, but could include the following suggestions:

- Regardless of the symbolic changes, the culture of the organization does not change, often due to a fear of making individuals in the dominant (power) groups uncomfortable
  - *Next step suggestion:* Plan books studies that focus on discussing taboo topics of identities to provide a basis for individuals to talk and venture outside of their comfort zone in a semi-structured way.

- Symbolic internal changes:
  - Officially changes policies and practices to focus on diversity inclusion; however, no real actionable change is observed within the culture of the organization
    - *Next step suggestion:* Evaluate the implementation of the changed policies that might have happened at the last level. Are the

policies being implemented? If not, how and why? With this bullet point, it is important to note that a variety of voices need to be at the table with equal input to influence the wider discussion.

- Self-identifies as an inclusive environment for all; however, some exclusionary practices are still in place

  - *Next step suggestion:* Identify exclusionary practices. (This is often done by coaches, outside evaluators, or internal stakeholders [e.g., employees, families].) In addition, evaluate the response to the exclusionary practices that are exposed. Is the response to ignore them or brush them off? Or is the response to understand the exclusionary practice with the goal of learning, growing, and changing as an organization to ensure that exclusion is not implemented?

- Intentional inclusive efforts (e.g., recruitment or bringing more views to the decision table); however, patterns of privilege are still apparent through "token" individuals placed at the table for image more than impact. *Example:* "We have a Black person on the ___ committee, so we are inclusive."

  - *Next step suggestion:* Critically analyze the committees, lead teachers, and other groups within the organization, at all levels, for tokenism. If there is tokenism, take steps to decrease tokenism, such as having reflective and open conversations about tokenism within the organization. In the classroom, tokenism can also appear in the curriculum that is implemented.

> **REFLECTION**
>
> As a leader, if you identify your organization at the Symbolic/Compliant Change level, what are your next steps? Why?

Identity/Affirming Change

The Identity/Affirming Change rating (4) includes the following specific aspects:

- Develops a wider understanding of power, privilege, and oppression as barriers to intentionally and effectively implementing equity-focused decision making, teaching, policies, and practices

- Internally processes and analyzes institutional power, privilege, and oppression

- Intentionally identifies as an inclusive, equity-focused organization by developing accountability measures in the active practice of dismantling dominant identity power and privilege

- Actively seeks to recruit and include members of historically marginalized identities; however, the power and privilege remain with the dominant identity groups. *Example:* Including individuals from historically oppressed identities "at the table" but not listening to their voices regarding decision making, teaching, practices, and policies.
- Expanding the definition of diversity and equity to include all oppressed identities

Level 4 is a level to strive for as an organization. Although Level 5 would be amazing for an organization to reach, both Levels 4 and 5 are where space is created for individuals to feel equitably welcomed, feel part of decision-making processes, and engage in honest conversations regarding power, privilege, and oppression. Therefore, if an organization self-identifies at the Identity/Affirming Change level, although there are next steps to take, many of the next steps are building on the already strong internal practices of the organization. Next steps could include the following suggestions:

- Develops a wider understanding of power, privilege, and oppression as barriers to intentionally and effectively implementing equity-focused decision making, teaching, policies, and practices
  - *Next step suggestion:* Continue to develop this strength by engaging in conversations and reflective practices.
- Internally processes and analyzes institutional power, privilege, and oppression
  - *Next step suggestion:* Continue to develop this strength by analyzing institutional power continuously. This internal processing should happen more than one time per year. It is recommended to engage in this process, intentionally, at least one time a month. This ensures that everyone centers equity in their work; understands the impact of power, privilege, and oppression; and explicitly reflects on issues in society that might affect the work of the program or organization.
- Intentionally identifies as an inclusive, equity-focused organization by developing accountability measures in the active practice of dismantling dominant identity power and privilege
  - *Next step suggestion:* Continue to develop this strength by developing and creating an accountability process that actively dismantles dominant identity power and privilege. Knowles et al. (2014), discussed this concept in the context of deny, distance, and dismantle, which is often the way dominant identities manage their identity. For this specific step, we focus on dismantling, which "reduces threat by relinquishing privilege" (p. 594). This is done by engaging in behaviors that reduce in-group privilege, such as recognizing harmful policies or recognizing inequities and see to remediate it.

- Actively seeks to recruit and include members of historically marginalized identities; however, the power and privilege remain with the dominant identity groups. *Example:* Including individuals from historically oppressed identities "at the table" but not listening to their voices regarding decision making, teaching, practices, and policies.
    - *Next step suggestion:* Continue to develop this strength by actively recruiting individuals from marginalized identities by reaching out to societies and organizational groups as a way to recruit and post available jobs. This could include the active recruitment of diverse employees; however, the voices may still not be listened to equally, as outlined in the previous change (symbolic change) level.
- Expanding the definition of diversity and equity to include all oppressed identities
    - *Next step suggestion:* Continue to develop this strength by expanding the definition of diversity and equity to include all oppressed identities. For example, according to the Charles T. Brown (2021):

Equity is the guarantee of fair treatment, access, opportunity, and advancement while at the same time striving to identify and eliminate barriers that have prevented the full participation of some groups. The principle of equity acknowledges that there are historically underserved and underrepresented populations and that fairness regarding these unbalanced conditions is needed to assist equality in the provision of effective opportunities to all groups.

> **REFLECTION**
>
> As a leader, if you identify your organization to be at the Identity/Affirming Change level, what are your next steps? Why?

Structural/Transformation Change

The Structural/Transformation Change rating (5) includes the following specific aspects:

- Commits to the intentional practice of organizational restructuring based on analysis of power- and privilege-embedded policies and practices.
- Restructures all aspects of the organization to ensure individuals from all historically marginalized identity groups fully participate in the organization (i.e., decision making, teaching, policies, and practices).
- Diversity and equity-focused practices become embedded organizational assets.

Table 5.2. Level 5 examples

Level 5 concept	Examples
Commits to the intentional practice of organization restructuring based on analysis of power- and privilege-embedded policies and practices.	All policies would include, for example, inclusive language (they/them) and clear statements of the CROWN Act.
Restructures all aspects of the organization to ensure individuals from all historically marginalized identity groups fully participate in the organization (i.e., decision making, teaching, policies, and practices).	The board of directors/leadership mirrors the diversity of the community. There is an open policy of providing feedback and "calling in" to all levels of leadership regarding equity-focused practices.
Diversity and equity-focused practices become embedded organizational assets.	Registration forms include a place for families to list their pronouns and preferred names. An American Sign Language teacher visits all the classes and teaches the students and teachers words to sign.
Commits to impact and actively engage in dismantling oppressive practices within the wider community. *Example:* Creating accountability strategies and rebuilding relationships previously damaged by power, privilege, and oppressive actions.	Teachers go out into their student's community for home visits and try to attend other community events. Teachers advocate for districtwide preschool screenings to have an interpreter and be located in areas families can access.

- Commits to impact and actively engage in dismantling oppressive practices within the wider community. *Example:* Creating accountability strategies and rebuilding relationships previously damaged by power, privilege, and oppressive actions.

Level 5 is the top of the Anti-Ism Scale and, therefore, the pinnacle of our goal to transform a program or classroom so that everyone feels brave, welcomed, and safe. However, being at a Level 5 does not mean there is no more work to be done. The work continues as organizations strive to stay at Level 5. Therefore, we provide a reflective table (see Table 5.2) to document the current status of Level 5.

> **REFLECTION**
>
> As a leader, if you identify your organization at the Structural/Transformative Change level, what are your next steps? Why?

COACHING TO THE ANTI-ISM SCALE

As already stated, one of the downsides we have seen in the use of the Anti-Ism Scale is that people consciously or unconsciously want to be "higher" and, therefore, are general or lack explicit connections to practices within the organization that connect to the points in the scale. Therefore, it is it imperative to be honest, reflective, and transparent through this process as a coach, leader, and as the wider program leadership team.

But what happens when a team is not fully honest with themselves or truthful throughout the process? It is important to remember that you cannot change anyone. They have to be ready to reflect, to be honest with themselves and their socialization, and to want to change. This is not something that can be forced, but something that needs to be guided. It is important to recognize, as the coach, that everyone in an organization is going to be at their own individual place on their growth journey while the organization as a whole is also on a growth journey.

Strategies to help the wider program be grounded in reality, versus an unintentional revisionist reality, include asking for policies and practices, asking for clear examples, and asking clear questions regarding the points in the Anti-Ism Scale columns. This is helpful regardless of where an organization places themselves initially. Diving into questions, as indicated earlier, is essential for the program employees to reflect and begin to actively engage in deep and honest conversations. Remember, the first "no" moving from left to right in the scale indicates the current level of the organization.

How does all of this work happen? The key is the person leading the work. Whether the person leading the work is the coach, a supervisor, or other leader, the individual (or group of individuals) needs to have knowledge and the ability and willingness to gently push the thinking of people. It is important to be able to ask probing questions, correct statements through calling in versus calling out, and be honest about one's own learning and growth journey focused on equity and diversity.

III

A Guide for Designing an Effective, Transformative DEIAB Program

6

Designing the Agenda

"It doesn't matter where you start. Only that you begin."
—Robin Sharma

Based on the planning team's (leadership) assessment, the initial topics for the first training workshop will be selected, which should be a whole-group training. The topic selection for the initial workshop should be a way to introduce the DEIAB work to the wider organization. To choose a topic, the leadership team should reflect on the questions already discussed but also answer this question: Where is the program ready to begin?

CASE STUDY: PROGRAM APPLES

In the case of Program Apples, their initial training focused on implicit biases and the importance of this work in the context of a classroom with racial homogeneity. The objectives for the first meeting were as follows:

1. Participants will be able to identify implicit biases in their personal and professional life.
2. Participants will be able to summarize the importance of equity work in early childhood classrooms, regardless of the student population.

As the leadership team plans the initial whole-group training, it is imperative to answer the 5W1H (who, what, why, where, when, and how) questions located in Figure 6.1. These questions will help the planning/leadership team organize and develop an agenda for the larger team training (Galiana, 2019).

WRITING WORKSHOP OBJECTIVES

Diving deeper into the "what" on the 5W1H questions, specifically when developing objectives for the workshops and/or overall learning, it is important to use action verbs because they can be measured. Words such as "understand" or "know" are not measurable and, therefore, should not be used for objectives or goals. For example, how do you know if someone understands? They will show you through matching, summarizing, or possibly explaining. Therefore, objectives are written with action verbs that can be measured.

A great resource to use to access applicable action verbs, based on the thinking skills needed to complete an objective, is to use the Bloom's taxonomy. In Figure 6.2, examples of verbs, based on the overarching thinking skills needed, are provided.

Furthermore, when writing objectives, another good practice is to use the ABCD Method, which ensures the learning outcomes are focused. The ABCD Method was developed by Heinrich et al. (1996). It stands for:

- *Audience.* Who are your learners?
- *Behavior.* Describe the task or behavior using action verbs that are observable.
- *Conditions.* Under what conditions? For example, what reference materials can the learner use?
- *Degree.* What degree of mastery is needed? Or how well must it be done based on, for example, speed, accuracy, or quality?

An example, in the context of DEIAB learning, is as follows: Educators (A) will articulate the impact of implicit biases (B) within the context of an early childhood learning environment using information gained from learning activities (C) in a reflective session with colleagues twice a year (D).

REFLECTION

Take time to write an objective using the ABCD Method for the work within your program.

Designing the Agenda

Organization's name _____	
Date _____	Event date _____

Questions to ask	Explanation
Who? (Who is this training for?)	When planning the initial group learning, all employees of the organization should be invited to the training because for true transformation to happen, all parties must be onboard. This includes the teaching staff, administrators, directors, food service workers, custodians, monitors, family support staff, and others who interact with the children and families daily. The reason why all of these positions are needed is because they are all a vital part of the team.
What? (What are the objectives?)	The objectives for the initial training should be focused on overall program goals surrounding the training. If training continues (we recommend that training be a yearlong or longer process), the objectives will be built from the specific needs of the program/organization. Providing the objectives for the training at the start of the workshop is helpful and sets the tone for the training.
When? (When will this happen?)	When will this occur during the school year calendar, and how long will the training be? We recommend, through the guidance of this book, that the process begins at the beginning of a program year and continues for at least 1 year, while also including information during the onboarding of new staff members. As far as the length of the actual workshop session, work within the constraints of your organization. A 1-hour training offers a brief exchange of information; however, it is hard to establish a sense of belonging in such a short amount of time. For more in-depth learning, a 3-hour training session is more appropriate to introduce a topic and begin to build a foundation. Even though 3 hours may seem like a significant amount of time, when you consider the activities, reflections, and small-group conversations that the training will include, those 3 hours are finished quickly. Regardless of "when" and "for how long," it is vital that these training sessions are interactive and hands-on.
Where? (Where will this take place?)	Finding a location that allows for interaction and movement should be a top priority. However, in our current reality, virtual workshops are more likely. In that case, make sure all participants have access to a computer and stable Internet.
Why? (Why is this training happening?)	Knowing why you are having the training will help you maintain focus on the task. Your team may recognize a need for DEIAB training, or the training might be mandated by the grant. Regardless of why the program/organization is participating in the DEIAB training, acknowledging the why provides a purpose and a purpose provides an end point to reach.
How? (What monetary and time commitments are needed?)	Training takes time and money. How will staff be compensated? If the program is bringing in an outside professional development provider, how will they be financially compensated? What other steps and procedures must take place before the training? Every organization has its own set of protocols and rules that must be followed.

Figure 6.1. 5W1H (who, what, why, where, when, and how) questions

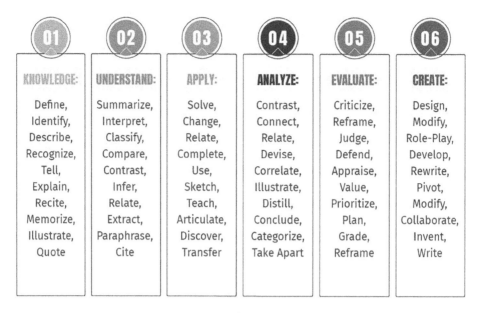

Figure 6.2. Bloom's taxonomy verbs. (From TeachThought Staff. [2018, December 17]. *100+ Bloom's Taxonomy Verbs for Critical Thinking*. TeachThought. https://www.teachthought.com/critical-thinking/blooms-taxonomy-verbs/; reprinted by permission.)

WHOLE-GROUP LEARNING TOPICS

Whole-group learning provides a shared experience and understanding for moving the work forward as a program or organization. The coach or leader needs to ensure that the whole-group learning creates a space for shared experiences, open thought processes, and developing a shared understanding of the topics to be learned.

When developing the objectives and agenda, it is also important to understand diversity in the context of early childhood. In Table 6.1, we

Table 6.1. What diversity is and is not

Diversity Is . . .	Diversity Is NOT . . .
Learning about personal backgrounds and experiences	Taught directly through a planned lesson, but rather is incorporated into the overall learning environment
Learning and acknowledging similarities and differences between and among people	A curriculum or a lesson plan
Seeing yourself (and others) represented throughout the learning environment	Cinco de Mayo, Black History Month, or Chinese New Year
Continually exposing children to activities, materials, and other experiences that destroy stereotypes	Dressing up in costumes, such as *headdresses, or eating Americanized "traditional" foods, such as tortillas
Appreciating and seeking differences of views, ways of solving problems, etc.	

*See text regarding discussion of asterisk.

provide examples of what diversity is and is not, which is a great reference to use as a coach or in the continued growth of a program.

Cultural Appropriation

Let's address the asterisk in Table 6.1. First, a headdress, or a Mulan, Pocahontas, or Moana costume (if you do not identify as that race/ethnicity), is cultural appropriation. Although there are many reasons why cultural appropriation is insensitive, it often enters early childhood classrooms around Halloween. As stated by Florida State University professor Elizabeth Scarbrough (2021):

> Examples of culturally appropriative Halloween costumes are—unfortunately—everywhere. . . . These costumes trade on a feature of cultural appropriation—outsiders of a particular culture use the resources (e.g., traditional clothing or perceived traditional clothing) of a culture that is not their own. But this alone doesn't get us all the way to cultural appropriation.
>
> Cultural appropriation is also about power. Notice that the Halloween costumes I mentioned earlier depict minoritized groups—this isn't accidental. Problematic cultural appropriation is a result of power imbalances. And in the United States, these imbalances often fall on racial lines. A White American dressing up as "pow wow princess" can be interpreted only within the context of settler colonialism. But (mis)appropriation is not always about race or ethnicity. There is a growing movement against wearing costumes that depict prison inmates, houseless folks, and people with mental illness as these costumes also trade on an imbalance of power. . . .
>
> The harm here is in stereotyping a culture (misrepresentation). Wearing this type of costume displays morally culpable ignorance about indigenous peoples and their practices. In our ignorance, we might also be wearing religious iconography in a flippant or disrespectful way (sacrilegious appropriation). We also run the risk of not just essentializing their culture but representing a living culture as a "something out of the past." (paras. 3, 4, and 5)

> **REFLECTION**
>
> Reflect on the definition of diversity in the context of your program. Then discuss the concept of cultural appropriation in the context of early childhood education.

Implicit Bias

Implicit biases are automatic associations, assumptions, and judgments. For the sake of understanding what an implicit bias is, read the following words. After you read each word, what is the very first image or word that you think of? Here are the words: soda pop, pie, animal, vegetable, toy. Maybe after reading the word soda pop, you had a picture of a neutral can of soda, or maybe you had a very specific liter of Pepsi in mind. This activity shows our tendency to make automatic associations, which are implicit biases. For example, in most cases, when someone says "peanut butter," the automatic association is jelly. That is an implicit bias.

This also happens when we discuss people, identities, or types of groups. Let's do the same activity with new words: scientist, doctor, nurse, teacher, truck driver, firefighter. What is the type of person you pictured with each word? What gender? What race? What age? Again, this displays our automatic attitudes, beliefs, and stereotypes that drive our preferences, which constitute implicit bias (Willen & Allan, 2021).

Another definition is that implicit biases are attitudes (positive and negative) toward people without our conscious knowledge. We all have implicit biases; it is something that is innate to humans. However, in the context of equity-focused education, we will primarily focus on the negative implicit biases that affect our development of inclusive learning environments as educators.

There are also explicit biases—the biases of which we are aware. For example, when explaining this topic, I (Thigpen) often use a soda analogy. I like the soda Sprite, but I do not like Sierra Mist or 7 Up. Since I am aware of my preference for Sprite, this is an explicit bias. However, if I was unaware of this preference, it would be an implicit bias.

An activity that is often used to help people understand implicit bias is the Harvard Implicit Association Test, which can be found by searching "Harvard Implicit Association Test" on any search engine. The Harvard Implicit Association Test activity demonstrates how we associate people with certain identities to have certain behaviors. In combination with completing the Harvard Implicit Association Test independently, we also encourage individuals to watch the video "Implicit Bias: Peanut Butter, Jelly and Racism," which was posted on YouTube on April 12, 2019, by Freedom Project WA.

> **REFLECTION**
>
> What surprised you about the Harvard Implicit Association Test and implicit bias video? Why?

Microaggressions

Microaggressions are the language of implicit bias. Specifically, microaggressions are the slights, insults, and put-downs that people receive daily due to their identity or intersectionality of identities. In school environments, children, families, and coworkers who have historically marginalized identities often deal with microaggressions at a higher rate than identities that are seen to have power and privilege in our society. To understand microaggressions further, watch a video often used in training that relates microaggressions to mosquito bites (search "Microaggression Mosquito Bites Clean Version").

Examples of microaggressions include the following:

- Telling BIPOC+ individuals, "I don't see color when I look at you." This denies their racial/ethnic experiences.

- Having low expectations for students who have individualized education programs (IEPs) or individualized family service plans (IFSPs).

- Treating boys and girls differently in a learning environment, such as viewing boys as more aggressive or seeing girls as weaker.
- Saying to young boys, "You are going to have to fight off the girls," or saying to young girls, "Do you have a boyfriend yet?" These statements make the assumption of heteronormativity.

Microaggressions create an environment that is toxic and unhealthy for learning. The intention of the person carrying out the microaggressions may not be to harm anyone. However, the impact of this exchange can be to harm the person receiving the microaggression (think back to intent versus impact). Repeated microaggressions affect a person's emotional, mental, and physical health and can lead to an increase in stress and possibly depression (Montoya, 2021). Even though the term is *micro*aggression, we want to highlight that, in fact, these put-downs and insults play a major role in how people feel in an environment.

> **REFLECTION**
>
> An activity that is often used to help people understand microaggressions is an activity from Epoch Education focused on recognizing microaggressions: https://epocheducation.com/wp-content/uploads/2021/03/microaggressions_tool_final-2021.pdf (Epoch Education, 2021). After completing the activity, reflect on the examples and checklist at the end of the document.

Hidden Curriculum

Building from microaggressions is the concept of hidden curricula. Hidden curriculum means allowing our implicit biases to be enacted through policies, classroom materials, and teaching practices. Putting our implicit biases into action in the classroom, consciously or unconsciously, shows the students and families which identities are valued and which are disvalued.

Officially, hidden curricula are "the unwritten, unofficial" rules that students learn in school (Thompson, 2017). These rules often teach children what behavior is expected in the classroom, such as raising a hand and waiting to be acknowledged before you speak. Children also learn whether or not they are valued. Referring back to the previous conversation regarding representation, for children to feel valued, children and families need to see themselves represented in the classroom through the language used, the materials in the dramatic play area, the books read, the music and movement encouraged, the lunch menu, the images used throughout the building, and the marketing materials put out by the wider community.

How do you start to recognize hidden curricula in learning environments? One way is to do an environmental scan of books. An activity we encourage programs to engage in is the process of analyzing the books in the learning environments. Do the books include any common stereotypes?

Are the books written by individuals who share the identity they are discussing or representing in the book? Are there a variety of books providing mirrors and windows in the classroom? Recognizing the hidden curriculum in your environment is a necessary step to make the environment a more inclusive and equitable place to learn.

> **REFLECTION**
>
> Analyze the books in your classroom library. Do they include any of the common stereotypes listed in Figure 6.3? After reviewing your books, reflect on other spaces in your classroom. Where is the hidden curriculum in your learning space? How are you providing mirrors, windows, and sliding glass doors for your children?

Consider author and illustrator background and perspective.
- If the book is not about people or events similar to the author or illustrator's background, what specifically recommends them as creators of the book?
- What is the author's attitude toward their story characters?
- Are the images accurate and do the illustrators respectfully render the people in the story?
- Do you have books reflecting a balanced range of author and illustrator identities and experiences?

Check illustrations.
- Look for stereotypes.

Common harmful/undermining stereotypes	
• Strong, independent girls and women are "manlike." • Latino men talk funny, are lazy, are gang members, or wear oversize sombreros. • African Americans are gang members or underemployed. • LGBTQ people are invisible or sexual predators. • Muslims are terrorists. • Muslim women are voiceless and passive.	• Book-loving or nonathletic boys and men are "effeminate." • Latina women are earth mothers or subservient. • People with disabilities are not independent or are to be pitied. • Poor people are invisible or depicted as passively needing help from others. • Indigenous peoples live in teepees, carry bows and arrows, or are half-naked in the winter.

Look for tokenism.
- Only seeing one person of any group in a book teaches children about who is more or less important.

Look for invisibility.
- What children do NOT see in books also teaches them about who matters and who doesn't matter in society.

Examples of groups of people who are often invisible in children's books or mainstream media	
• Families who live in rural areas • Blue-collar workers • Musicians, artists, and writers • Families with two dads or two moms • Single mothers or fathers	• Homeless families • Families with an incarcerated parent • People of Arab decent and/or families who practice Islam • Transgender adults and children

Figure 6.3. Selecting antibias children's books.

Figure 6.3. *(continued)*

Check the storyline and the relationships between people.
- Does the storyline carry biases?
- Are White people (White males) the central figures?
- To gain acceptance, does a historically marginalized character need to do something extraordinary?
- Who typically causes the problem? Who typically resolves it?
- Does your collection of books balance various people in "doer" roles?

Look at messages about varying lifestyles.
- Are negative value judgments implied about ways of life that are different from those in the dominant culture?
- Does the setting reflect current life or past assumptions about life?

Consider the impact on children's self and social identities.
- Do the books reinforce or counteract messages that teach children to feel inferior or superior because of their skin color, gender, family income, able-bodiedness, or type of family structure?
- Do the children in your classroom see windows, mirrors, and sliding glass doors?

Watch for "loaded words."
- A word is loaded when it in any way demeans people or makes people invisible because of any of their identities (e.g., "all men" meaning everyone, including women).
- Examples of adjectives applied to people of color that carry racist messages include "savage," "primitive," "superstitious," "backward," "inscrutable," and "treacherous." Always consider the context in which a word is used and to whom it applies.
- Avoid sexist language:

Use this:	Instead of this:
• Community	• Brotherhood
• Firefighters	• Firemen
• Ancestors	• Forefathers
• Chairperson	• Chairman
• Mail carrier	• Postman
• Police officer	• Policeman

Great websites to check out:
- https://diversebooks.org/
- http://hereweeread.com/

As you might have noticed, this section has primarily focused on assumptions, actions, or implementation practices that are more negative or deficit based. However, that is not where we leave the conversation. To continue forward momentum, the funds of knowledge and approaching children and families through a strengths-based mindset are essential.

Funds of Knowledge

The term "funds of knowledge," or human capital, refers to the skills that students and parents bring in the form of education, work experience, and language knowledge that make individuals productive at home, school, and work (Moll et al., 1992). Funds of knowledge focus on the strengths that children and family bring with them into the learning environment. When we focus on students' and families' funds of knowledge, we ensure an equity-focused approach from a strengths-based perspective (as opposed to a deficit-based perspective). Essentially, we do not want to focus on what the child or family may be lacking, but rather on what they bring into the classroom as background, experiences, stories, knowledge, and more. Remember, families do not need educators to fix them because they are not broken.

Strengths-Based Approach

By basing our work on developing and cultivating our own strengths-based approach, it is important to ground ourselves in the principles of the strengths-based approach (Hammond, 2010), which are as follows:

1. Everyone possesses a uniqueness that helps them evolve and move along their journey.
2. What receives attention or focus becomes what the client strives for and eventually becomes a reality.
3. Be careful with your words and language.
4. Accept change: Our lives and our world are ever evolving.
5. Support others as authentically as you can.
6. The client is the storyteller of their own life.
7. Build upon what you know and experience to dream about the future.
8. Capacity building has multiple facets and organization. Be flexible.
9. Be collaborative. Be adaptive and value differences.

> **REFLECTION**
>
> What role do you think your implicit bias has played in your ability to see strengths in others?

As noted in this chapter, there are many things to consider when planning for this work, and initially, it is on the shoulders of the leadership team. However, although this work may be challenging, it is needed as the program and individuals continually learn, grow, and change.

7

Initial Group Learning

"Yes, I am imperfect and vulnerable and sometimes afraid, but that doesn't change the truth that I am also brave and worthy of love and belonging."

—Brené Brown

Coaches (leadership), it is time to engage with the group, which begins with developing a sense of belonging. This can be done in a multitude of ways, but here, we will walk through our go-to strategy known as the Morning Meeting, based on the Responsive Classroom Framework.

MORNING MEETING

You would be hard-pressed to find a room full of individuals who actually like icebreakers, but there is a point to icebreakers: to initially and quickly create a shared experience to build closer connections (Rise, 2021). One way we create this shared experience at the beginning of a group workshop is by embedding what the classroom management system Responsive Classroom (2016) calls a "Morning Meeting." Every time the group meets, the meeting should begin with this shared experience to center participants in the community.

In essence, a Morning Meeting has four parts:

1. Greeting
2. Share

3. Game
4. Message

Greeting

The Morning Meeting begins with all of the participants standing in a circle. However, if the workshop is virtual, this can still be completed in breakout rooms. The greeting includes a low-risk way to say hello to everyone in the room, such as a wave. As part of this process, it is imperative that the participants hear their names from each other and not the leader, which creates a sense of community. For example, if I am standing next to Jacinda and Jacinda is next to Nathan, the exchange would start like this:

Waving to Jacinda, I would say, "Hi, I'm Anni." Jacinda would wave back to me and say, "Hi, Anni. I am Jacinda." I would respond by saying, "Hi, Jacinda."

Jacinda would then turn to Nathan and wave, saying, "Hi, I am Jacinda." Nathan would return the greeting by saying, "Hi, Jacinda. I am Nathan." Jacinda would respond by saying, "Hi, Nathan."

Note: If the group members do not know the people standing next to them, have them introduce themselves before beginning the greeting.

Continue this process around the circle, room, or virtual breakout room until everyone has heard their name stated in the environment from another community member. This process creates a sense of belonging and provides an opportunity for much-needed social interactions (Allen-Hughes, 2013).

If you have limited time and are completing this session virtually, another greeting we use is to have people find three things around them that describe who they are as an individual. They are then prompted to share the three objects with a group of peers in a breakout room or in the larger room. Through the process of coming together and building community, participants are able to engage in interactions and begin to establish collaborative relationships.

Sharing

The share portion of the Morning Meeting is next. The goal of the share is to create a further sense of belonging. There are two ways to complete the share. One way is for every person in the group to share one word or sentence about a like or dislike, which does not need to connect to the overall topic. Such as, "What is your favorite color?" or "What is your least favorite food?"

Another way to complete the share is to have three volunteers share something about their day, week, or life. Often, these shares are about vacations, happy family news, and other exciting events in participants' lives. After each share, the leader will turn to the group and say, "Okay, now it is our turn to ask three questions. Who has a question about this share?" Inevitably, this turns into a time of smiles, shared joy, and a shared experience.

Game

Next in the Morning Meeting agenda is a game. A good go-to icebreaker, especially for individuals who are more introverted, is known as the "Switch Sides If" game.

"Switch Sides If" begins with splitting the group into two groups on either side of the room. Ask the participants to take note of the people they are starting with on their side of the room. Then, begin the game. Provide about 5–10 "Switch Sides If" scenarios. For example, in the Midwest, a common go-to is to switch sides if you are a Cubs fan (Cubs vs Cardinals). This often gets people smiling and laughing. Toward the end of your five to 10 scenarios, begin to bring it back to the topic at hand, but still keep it fun. On the topic of diversity, you might say, "Switch sides if you are over the age of 40" or "Switch sides if you speak more than one language." The benefit of this game is that it is not only fun and active, but also people can choose if they want to "out" an identity or keep it private—no one is calling them out in this game.

At the end of the game, ask participants to look at who is on their side now; inevitably, the groups are different than the starting groups. This is an easy, low-risk icebreaker that helps all participants understand that they are both alike and different. At the end of the game, you might state, "The group we started with is not the group we ended with because of the uniqueness of our identities and innate diversity." The idea of unique individuals making a whole environment is a concept that can continually be referred to throughout the DEIAB training and work. Essentially, we are all individuals with our own unique likes, dislikes, backgrounds, and experiences, but we are also part of this larger community that focuses on the Platinum Rule. Grounding the work in this simple exercise of individuals within a community will help in the growth, learning, and change process of the group.

Another icebreaker is "Would You Rather?" This activity can be done in person or virtually, using an interactive website such as Kahoot! or Mentimeter. An example question is "Would you rather vacation at a beach or go hiking?" When completing this activity in person, you will have people stand and pick a side based on their response to the question. The questions can be about various topics such as the questions used in "Switch Sides If." To complete this activity virtually, have participants vote through an interactive website.

Regardless of the game or icebreaker, it is important that the same message is emphasized: No one is truly the same as anyone else, and as educators, it is our role to create a welcoming environment regardless of values or beliefs.

> **REFLECTION**
>
> Based on your organization, what activities do you think would be best for developing a sense of belonging?

Message

The message is the final part of the Morning Meeting. The message often revolves around the objectives for the session, which are written using the ABCD Method introduced in Chapter 6. In addition, the message portion of the Morning Meeting is also a great time to introduce or review the community agreements.

COMMUNITY AGREEMENTS

Community agreements are norms or rules of engagement that are provided as a way to build a safe space for learning. The community agreements we often use are as follows:

- Be brave.
- Be honest.
- Be vulnerable.
- Be okay with nonclosure.
- Have a beginner's mindset.
- Assume good intent.
- Speak from the "I."

After stating the agreements, we leave room for participants to agree to them or add more. Often, confidentiality is added by a participant and agreed upon by the group.

What do each of the community agreements mean?

Be Brave

This means that participants are asked to approach the topics included in DEIAB training, which are often taboo and sometimes contentious, with courage. Be brave to ask questions and interact, even if it is uncomfortable.

Be Honest

This means that group members should be honest with themselves. Are the participants truly being honest about their implicit biases or prejudices? Being honest with oneself is the first step in the reflection and growth process.

Be Vulnerable

Often this means being okay with asking questions that may seem ignorant. Being vulnerable means putting yourself out there with the goal of learning and addressing feelings or emotions that may arise.

Be Okay With Nonclosure

This is an important agreement because participants will often leave with more questions than answers, which is part of the learning and growing process. When you leave with nonclosure, it provides a place to start your own guided discovery regarding topics or concepts.

Have a Beginner's Mindset

As more teachers and educators are participating in equity training and gaining knowledge on various topics, it is essential for all individuals to approach each session and concept with a beginner's mindset. This allows for individuals to engage and to view information with a new perspective, rather than assuming they already know all the information about a specific topic discussed.

Assume Good Intent

As a group, we want to assume that everyone is asking questions and entering the space with good intentions.

Speak From the "I"

Your experience, my experience, and your neighbor's experience are all different. Reinking, as a White woman, does not speak for all White women. Thigpen, as a Black woman, does not speak for all Black women. Neither of us speaks for all women. Therefore, when engaging in discussions, it is important to use "I" as in, "I feel threatened when I enter the grocery store," as opposed to saying, "We feel threatened when entering the grocery store." Your experience is your experience and your experience only. However, coaches can discuss generalizations based on research throughout the training as a way to provide context.

DEFINE YOUR WHY

After the performing the icebreakers and setting community agreements, it is important to ask participants to define their "why" and to write it down. For example: Why are they at the workshop? Why do they feel this work is important or not important? Why is it important to create inclusive environments?

Once individual whys are completed, the leadership team should share the program why, which is: Why is this training taking place? The answer is based on the work the leadership team completed to plan the first session.

Once the whys are written and possibly spoken aloud, it is time to complete the Social Identity Wheel and discuss the participants' intersectionality of identities. Afterward, the topic that was chosen for the agenda will be presented in an interactive way that considers the adult learning theory and provides opportunities for the learning to be applied to each participant.

CASE STUDY: PROGRAM APPLES

The first session with Program Apples was spread over several weeks due to the allotted amount of time provided for each session. It was important to develop a sense of belonging at the beginning because the staff came to the session with varying feelings and perspectives regarding the DEIAB work that was going to be introduced. How do we know there were varying feelings? We engaged in a "Do Now" activity (an activity we call "One Word"). As the staff members arrived, we asked them to anonymously report, through Mentimeter, how they were coming to the session, specifically regarding mind and body. Many participants responded with "angry," "uninterested," "tired," and "overwhelmed." Other responses included "interested," "skeptical," "ready to learn," and "excited." It was important to consider all of the responses to understand where the group was starting.

After developing a sense of belonging in the group, we eased into the Social Identity Wheel activity. We discussed the use of the word "Caucasian" and replacing it with "White" since Caucasian means "the most beautiful" (Jewell, 2020). We also discussed the word "straight" and replacing it with "heterosexual" because of the implications of being the opposite of straight. In Merriam-Webster, the antonyms of straight include "devious," "serpentine," "unbecoming," "corrupt," "perverted," and the list goes on. Despite our best intentions as professional development providers, the first session was not completely smooth. When participants were asked to anonymously enter their overall feelings and thoughts of the workshop, the word cloud that was created through those anonymous entries on Mentimeter still included words such as "angry." However, there were also words such as "interested," "intrigued," and "curious." That did not mean our work stopped. It meant that we needed to continue the process of relationship building to develop a positive rapport for learning together, as well as understanding the backgrounds and experiences of the teachers.

CONCLUDING THE MEETING

A concluding activity that we often use for virtual professional development is an activity in Mentimeter that we call "One Word," which was described earlier in the case study. One reason we like this activity is because it allows participants to anonymously share their thoughts, feelings, and perceptions. Figure 7.1 shows a Mentimeter word cloud from a training we did with Program Apples. As you can see, there was growth since the first meeting reported in the case study. The way a word cloud works is that the more a word is entered by the participants, the bigger it becomes.

CASE STUDY: PROGRAM APPLES

Based on the Mentimeter word cloud shown in Figure 7.1, the discussion we had with the group was as follows:

> As you can see in this word cloud, you, as a group, understand that change is part of this process—the process of engaging in diversity and equity work in the early childhood classroom. It is also nice to see you are hopeful. Maybe you are hopeful for future

Figure 7.1. Mentimeter word cloud.

generations. Maybe you are hopeful as a Program working toward transformative implementation practices to include all students and families. Regardless of why you are hopeful, we appreciate your participation in this activity. However, we also want to point out other words in the word cloud that may not be as prominent but are still very important because your colleagues have varying degrees of comfort or acknowledgement of this work. For example, as you can see, the words "unsettled" and "depressing" are valid and important feelings to acknowledge and process. You may have chosen the one word of "depressing" based on new knowledge you learned today about historically marginalized individuals, or you may have chosen the one word of "unsettled" because of a feeling of discomfort about potential future changes. It is important to note that many times some of these feelings are based in a fear of losing the known and a fear of the unknown future. What changes will be made? Will the changes be within your locus of control? It is also important to remember our community agreement of "being okay with nonclosure." The feelings of "unsettled" or "depressing" may stem from a sense of not having answers—leaving with nonclosure. That is part of this work and provides a place for your future growth as an individual or maybe as a team.

In-person conclusion activities can also use the Mentimeter word cloud; however, verbally stating the word out loud can also impact the group work, and you lose the anonymity. When everyone hears the word and sees the person saying it, it adds more meaning to the word within the context of who that individual is in the group. Other types of concluding activities that can be done in person include the following:

- *Square, Triangle, Circle:* State four things that make sense or "square" with you, three things that you are going to try, and two things that are "circling" around in your head (e.g., What are you thinking or wondering as you prepare to leave?).

- *Draw a Picture:* Draw a picture of what is going through your mind right now in relation to the knowledge you gained from today's session.

- *Tweet It:* Write a tweet to summarize your learning. As a reminder, a tweet is 280 characters, which includes symbols, letters, numbers, and spaces.

- *Questions:* Write two questions and share with a peer. Write the answer to the questions or share with the group for more clarification based on the information learned during the workshop.

- *Journal:* Establish a personal journal, team journal, or peer journal. A personal journal is used for your own reflections. A team journal is used to share thoughts in a collective format. A peer journal is used to discuss and process your learning in an asynchronous format with a peer.

THE NEXT STEPS

At the end of the first session, ask all of the participants to complete two items:

- Ask for volunteers to be part of a diverse workgroup to plan, implement, and provide future workshops on programwide implementation practices. We have found that when the whole group is asked, rather than asking specific people, the individuals who volunteer may surprise you and the work seems to be more focused on true change.

- Ask participants to evaluate where they believe the organization is on the Anti-Ism Scale in an anonymous survey. It may also be helpful to add an optional open-ended question for participants to explain their rating. This can be done using a Google survey (see Figure 7.2) or a paper survey if done in person. Whichever survey format you use, it should be stressed that all individuals need to truthfully complete the survey and stay anonymous (see https://forms.gle/NLXXPLFapkwT252U6).

Finally, in Figure 7.3, we provide an example agenda that outlines everything discussed in this chapter for the initial group learning workshop.

REFLECTION

Based on the two parts of the case study presented in this chapter, what would you, as a coach, suggest as next steps? What might you do next to help in learning and change?

Evaluate where you believe the organization is on the Anti-Ism Scale.

○ Exclusive (1)

○ Passive/tolerant (2)

○ Symbolic/compliant change (3)

○ Identify/affirming change (4)

○ Structural/transformative change (5)

Please explain your rating. (Why did you select the rating above?)

_____

Figure 7.2. Anti-Ism Scale survey example.

Morning meeting • Greeting • Share • Game • Message (goals and community agreements)	20–30 minutes
Social Identity Wheel Activity	10–20 minutes
Topic introduction	5 minutes

Video
   Examples:
     • Video on microaggressions (Mosquito Bites)
     • Video on implicit bias (Peanut Butter Jelly)
	2–10 minutes

Small-group reflection	Varies
Activity (reflection questions about activity)	Varies
Exit survey/questionnaire	2–5 minutes

Figure 7.3. Agenda outline. (From Reinking, A. & Thigpen, L. [2021]. Agenda Outline; reprinted by permission.)

8

Equity and Diversity Workgroup

"Diversity: the art of thinking independently together."
—Malcolm Forbes

Why do we need a Diversity Workgroup? The reason for developing a Diversity Workgroup is to enable transformation of the organization by having a small group of individuals analyze, critically reflect, and plan for changes and improvements. The Diversity Workgroup should include, if possible, individuals from different levels of the organization. The purpose of the Diversity Workgroup is for individuals to come together, carry the voices of their coworkers, and create an environment where all voices are included. Often, the Diversity Workgroup is composed of volunteers.

WHAT IS NEEDED FOR A DIVERSITY WORKGROUP?

- *Volunteers.* The work will be more focused and action based when individuals volunteer to be part of the work rather than being "volun-told."
  - *What if no one volunteers?* Continue the process as a whole group until there is a group of people who are ready to form a workgroup. If anyone feels pushed or pressured into participating in a group leading any work, including diversity work, the end result may not be advantageous for the program or organization.

- *Diversity.* Although volunteers are generally requested, at times, some individuals may need to be asked directly to ensure that all levels of the organization are represented and to ensure that different identities on the Social Identity Wheel are represented at the table. The process of creating the group should not be one of ticking off boxes on a checklist, but rather, it should be conscious of the homogeneity or heterogeneity of the group.
- *Commitment.* Time commitment is a critical piece of this workgroup. It will take time, research, and dedication to ensure that the materials and resources provided are current, as well as to develop programwide implementation plans for coworkers to use in their own learning environments.
- *Support.* The Diversity Workgroup needs to feel supported through both monetary support (stipend) and access to leadership support. Leadership support means that the leadership team (e.g., supervisor, director) supporting the work follows through with coaching and supervising to ensure the equity-focused resources are implemented.

Once the Diversity Workgroup is put together focusing on the four previously listed needs of a diversity group and a meeting schedule is designed, the benefits of the group will surface. Benefits that could surface include hearing various perspectives that represent the organization's different positions and a sense of community in learning and planning equity-focused implementation practices for learning environments.

Hearing various perspectives while planning and learning in the Diversity Workgroup is inevitable because each person comes to the group with their own position and identity. This positionality can be simulated in an activity that I (Thigpen) often have preservice teachers complete in a course. I place an object on a table in the front of the room and have each student draw the object from the perspective they have of the object from their seat. The finished product is a collage that includes all of the various drawings of the object from different perspectives. The goal of the activity is to help preservice teachers understand that we can look at the same thing and have different perspectives or focus. Bringing this concept into the work of the Diversity Workgroup is important because including various perspectives allows for a more accurate assessment of the organization, which in turn allows for needed planning and learning (Ellemers & Rink, 2016).

In addition, as already stated several times throughout this book, this work is hard. Bringing a group of people with one goal (equity-focused education) together can be quite different when perspectives differ on how to move forward in the work. Therefore, it is essential to build a sense of community between and among the members of the Diversity Workgroup. Ideas might include sharing their Social Identity Wheel, sharing their "why" for this work, or even just completing a simple icebreaker bingo game. The goal of this essential work (i.e., developing a community) will have a long-lasting impact on the work the Diversity Workgroup is able to develop and disseminate.

BENEFITS OF A DIVERSE WORKGROUP

Building a diverse Diversity Workgroup benefits the overall organization. The varied perspectives allow for increased productivity and creativity due to the variety of cultural and lived experiences that each person brings. Encouraging individuality allows for people to share their ideas and build upon each other's thoughts to problem-solve.

Having a diverse team also allows for discussions that are based in cultural relevance based on experiences and not assumptions of reality. For example, having bilingual staff in your organization is an asset to families who may not speak fluent English. Furthermore, organizations with a diverse team that is supportive often receive a positive reputation for being a place that is inclusive. This positive reputation further attracts potential employees and families that want to be part of the positivity.

CASE STUDY: PROGRAM APPLES

In Program Apples, volunteers were asked to lead the diversity and equity work after the first training. Four teachers and five paraprofessionals volunteered. There was one Black male and one Latinx female, and the remainder of volunteers were White females, all with various years of experience in early childhood education. When we, as the outside coaches, reflected with the leadership team on who volunteered to be part of the Diversity Workgroup, the leadership team shared that they were surprised about some of the volunteers. They were surprised because one volunteer was someone new to the program and another was someone who was soft-spoken in the program and never appeared to be someone interested in this work. They were also surprised that diversity was achieved by simply asking for volunteers.

POSITIVE GROUP DYNAMICS

Integral to the development of positive group dynamics is designing an environment where everyone feels as though they their identity is fully seen, their voices are truly heard, and their opinions or ideas are discussed (Hall, 2014). So, how do you create this idyllic positive group dynamic, especially when discussing potentially stress-inducing or conflict-ridden topics such as those discussed as part of DEIAB?

Although there are many ways to develop a positive group identity, we will specifically discuss the process we use in our workshops. This process may not work for your program, and that is okay. We encourage you to use this example as a launching point for brainstorming best practices based on the individuals in your program. However, when planning, it is important to constantly reflect on thoughts that might pop up such as, "They wouldn't like it" or "I don't think it will work." This mindset is usually a sign of personal insecurities (Annette, 2019). So, do the activity you initially thought of and push yourself and your colleagues outside of your comfort zones. Yes, this process is going to be uncomfortable and stressful, as we have already discussed. However, in the end, the process of change will benefit not only the children in your program but also the wider school and community environments.

BARRIERS TO CREATING A DIVERSE WORKGROUP

Developing a Diversity Workgroup is not always as easy as described in Program Apples. There are potential barriers.

First, what if your staff is not diverse? Although organizations should strive to have employees who have different identities based on the Social Identity Wheel, this is not always the case. The elementary teaching population is still predominantly White, Christian, and female, leaving some educational organizations with no Black or Brown teachers and no male teachers (Aronson & Meyers, 2020).

> **REFLECTION**
>
> Do the staff demographics reflect the families or community that you serve? Why or why not?

One question that is often asked when discussing diversifying a team is "How?" Here are some guiding tips:

1. Analyze your recruitment practices. For example, do you advertise to local historically Black colleges and universities (HBCUs), community colleges, and diverse high schools? If you truly want to change your organization's diversity, you must reach out to include voices that are not often represented. Included in this strategy is evaluating the marketing materials disseminated by the program. Do the images and words display inclusivity or exclusivity?

2. Consider the history and demographics of the location of your organization. For example, is your organization located in a town that was affected by redlining or White flight? What is the perceived community relationship with Black and Brown peopled? What are the community attitudes toward families who are of lower socioeconomic status?

3. Celebrate the diversity that you do have. All organizations may not be diverse based on race, but considering other identities on the Social Identity Wheel, your organization could include people with many diverse identities, lifestyles, and hobbies. Remember, diversity means differences.

A second barrier is placing the burden of discussing diversity on Black and Brown professionals as a way to educate "everyone else." Remember, it is not the responsibility of BIPOC+ people to educate White people on diversity. Black and Brown people cannot be expected to carry the added burden of representing all people who share their identity, in addition to coping with the constant barrage of microaggressions from colleagues, speaking up on injustices, and having to "tone down" their culture to be accepted. The burden of diversifying your organization belongs to your organization.

Another barrier is the discriminatory practices that are often embedded into society that are often not recognized by privileged identities until pointed out. Remember, being part of this planning team is a choice. Therefore, allowing all people an opportunity to participate allows a space for diverse voices. However, when a BIPOC+ professional (or a person with a historically marginalized identity) decides to participate, here are suggestions to create an inclusive environment (Hunt, 2020):

- Do listen.
- Don't keep saying "I'm sorry" and putting the burden on "that" colleague to respond. (Do stay empathic and compassionate.)
- Don't ask to be educated on racism (or sexism, ageism, or any ism). (Do take the time to educate yourself.)
- Don't take up space with how you feel burdened. It's not your time. (Do listen and allow your colleague this time and/or space.)
- Don't ask if you have done anything to discriminate against a group of people. (Do be reflective about your words and actions toward people.)
- Don't force anyone to share if they don't want to. (Do ask for volunteers and show respect to those who decline.)

Although these recommendations were made to address racism, they can be used to support all staff who identify as part of a marginalized group.

The fourth barrier to creating a diverse Diversity Workgroup comes back to the concept of tokenism. As your program takes the steps to recruit and employ people from diverse backgrounds, it must also challenge the internal motives to ensure that they are not just trying to fill a diversity quota.

Being the only person with an identity of a marginalized group can be uncomfortable and isolating (Ali, 2020). The following poem vocalizes these thoughts and was written by Thigpen as she reflected on this work.

No One Here Looks Like Me

Standing in the doorway, scanning the room,
I am faced with the reality that no one here looks like me.
White, middle class, females make up the majority in my education field.
My identity differs from the dominant culture, so as an outsider I feel.
This is my situation as an outsider time and time again.
How do I respond to being "the only one" — what are my options?
Do I leave because I do not want to sit through another training and witness
 another White person process their White guilt?
Do I nod my head to show empathy as people are shocked by the realizations of
 marginalized communities that policies built?
Do I sit there and try to disconnect from these conversations in order to protect
 my mental health?
Do I open my mouth and share my reality based on my identity in hopes to
 educate someone else?
The environments that I enter in as an educator do not display the representation
 that I need.
So once again, here I am, distracted and disengaged by the fact that no one here
 looks like me.

—Laycee Thigpen, 2021

This poem speaks to the reality many educators feel who do not fit into the historically molded idea of what an educator looks like. Although an employee works for the organization and shares similarities due to being an employee, the person may still feel like an outsider and different from the group. As a response to this feeling, the employee may self-isolate or be reluctant to participate.

REFLECTION

What are your initial thoughts after reading the poem? Does this poem speak to you? How? What can you do to support this person? What are you willing to do to support this person?

PLANNING FOR PROGRAMMATIC CHANGES

After addressing the barriers and establishing a Diversity Workgroup, planning for programmatic change can begin. The workgroup must think about the logistics, such as setting the meeting schedule, reflecting on purposeful language, and setting goals.

Regarding scheduling, we suggest that all individuals in the Diversity Workgroup meet twice a month to begin. Once the DEIAB implementation has begun, the workgroup should have a monthly meeting for check-ins. The check-ins could include feedback they are receiving from coworkers or their own personal experiences with implementing programmatic change.

ESTABLISHING A PURPOSE AND STATEMENT

At the first meeting, it is important to establish roles. Who will take notes? Who will keep the committee progressing through goals? Who will keep a running list of to-dos? How the roles are assigned can depend on the program and the consensus of the Diversity Workgroup. Does the staff want to be assigned a different role each time the group meets? Does the staff want to be assigned roles or volunteer for roles? There is not one way to fill the roles; it truly depends on your group.

When the Diversity Workgroup first meets, there are two initial goals: 1) develop a working purpose and 2) develop a programwide diversity statement.

A purpose statement is just that—the purpose of why the Diversity Workgroup is meeting. An effective strategy we often use to determine the Diversity Workgroup purpose is to engage in an activity we call "Throw Me Your Idea." This is not a new activity, but we add in a fun twist.

In person, we provide each member of the workgroup with a pad of sticky notes. We set a timer for 2 minutes with the instructions to write one word per sticky note that describes their "why" or their view of the workgroup purpose. At the end of the 2 minutes, they crumple or ball up each of the sticky notes and literally throw them to the front of the room. Once all of the words on the sticky notes are thrown to the front of the room, we take turns finding one, opening it up, reading it, adding it to a list at the front of the room, and discussing the words as a group. Through this process, words start to form categories or ideas that are shared by the group as the purpose of the workgroup. There are multiple benefits to this type of activity, including group members getting up and moving around (active), hearing the words aloud (shared voice), discussing each word (everyone being heard), and, in the end, with the guidance of the coach, developing a purpose statement.

Virtually, the Diversity Workgroup can complete this activity by using Jamboard or IdeaBoardz. However, members are not able to "throw" their words and ideas, but a discussion can still occur.

Although "Throw Me Your Idea" is one way to develop a purpose, as you will read in the case study, Program Apples based both their purpose and diversity statements in antibias education (ABE).

According to Doeing (2019), an organization's diversity statement is "a written explanation of its commitment to diversity, equity, and inclusion for its employees and customers. It tells stakeholders how diversity fits into

Positive Words for Diversity Statement	
Authentic	Empower
Inclusive	Intentional
Purposeful	Accept

Figure 8.1. Positive words for diversity statement. (*Source:* Kelly, 2018.)

your organization's mission and values." The title of the diversity statement should stand out; it should say something other than "diversity statement" (Brew, 2020). According to Heaslip (2020), your statement should answer the following questions:

1. What does diversity, equity, and inclusion (DEI) mean to your organization?
2. Why does DEI matter to us both presently and for the future?
3. How can we approach DEI now, and what activities can we plan for the future?

By answering these questions, a diversity statement can be created that suits your program and can be easily comprehended. Your statement should include information connecting to your program's established mission and include positive words (listed in Figure 8.1) (Kelly, 2018).

If your program already has a diversity statement, you might want to consider revising it. A best practice for your organization is to revisit the current diversity statement every year and make changes if needed.

Having a diversity statement is not enough. The diversity statement is not just an item your Diversity Workgroup checks off as completed,

REFLECTION

Reflect on the diversity statement of your organization using the following questions (Brew, 2020):

1. How long ago was the diversity statement written?
2. Is the language current and inclusive?
3. How easy is it for employees and others to find?

but it should truly embody the direction of your program. A diversity statement is not going to make your program more diverse. A diversity statement is not going to change the way historically marginalized people feel being "one of the few" in an environment where they are not the majority. A diversity statement is just a statement. When action is added that supports your diversity statement, then transformation can happen.

CASE STUDY: PROGRAM APPLES

At the first meeting of the Diversity Workgroup, the group centered their work on the current mission and vision of the program, which was a great way to center the conversation. Next, they took time to write down every word they thought of regarding diversity in relation to their program and their personal reason for joining the group. By the end of this brainstorming session, there were multiple poster papers on the wall with words, phrases, and thoughts. Once the lists were created, it was time to look for common themes. With our guidance, overarching themes were created. These were themes that the Diversity Workgroup agreed upon as areas of focus and importance for the wider program and the DEIAB work. From there, we guided the development of a working purpose for the group and a diversity statement.

This work did not happen instantaneously, but rather over the course of two 1-hour sessions, with time in between the sessions for the group members to reflect, brainstorm further, and come back to the group with working statements. In the end, the working purpose designed by the group was as follows: The goal of this committee is to focus on a programwide response to implement change focused on antibias education.

The diversity statement for the program that was developed was as follows: Program Apples is a community-based program that accepts and celebrates all educators, families, caregivers, and children regardless of their identity. As a program, we are committed to creating an environment where everyone feels a sense of belonging, everyone feels empowered to grow and learn, and everyone is welcomed. Overall, our goal is to implement impactful change focused on antibias education.

Program Apples was able to get their diversity statement approved and on their website.

ANTI-ISM SCALE ORGANIZATION RATING

After establishing the purpose of the Diversity Workgroup and developing or approving the diversity statement, it is time to discuss the Anti-Ism Scale ratings. Using the information from the initial whole-program meeting, specifically the survey data regarding the Anti-Ism Scale, the Diversity

Workgroup should discuss the ratings. Some good guiding questions include the following:

1. What do the data indicate?
2. What is the average score among all of the staff members?
3. What is the reasoning provided for ratings?
4. Are there concepts missing from the data? Are there concepts that the group did not know about until reading the survey responses?
5. Does the staff rating match the administration's rating?
6. Comparing the administration's assessment and the staff assessment of the organization, based on the Anti-Ism Scale, what are the commonalities and what are the differences? Why?
7. What challenges do you perceive your organization has in creating a fully inclusive environment?
8. How diverse is your organization? (Think beyond race.)

This list of questions is not exhaustive. It is assumed that program-specific questions will be raised by the Diversity Workgroup. Once the discussion starts to come to an end, with the guidance of the coach, it is time to provide a "final" rating on the Anti-Ism Scale for your organization. This rating will provide a starting point for the Diversity Workgroup and wider program.

As coaches, we suggest going with the lowest rating that the group is comfortable with based on the feedback from the staff and the leadership ratings. The reason we provide this recommendation is that the program wants to make sure nothing is seen as "okay" or "not important" and therefore skipped over in the scale. If the entire workgroup cannot come to a decision, the final decision is made by the coach or administrator leading the work, with the understanding that a compromise is often needed.

After deciding on an organization rating, it is time to dig in and do the work of action planning and action.

SETTING GOALS

Based on the Anti-Ism Scale organization rating, the workgroup can start discussing both short- and long-term goals. It is good to have both types of goals because it is motivating to feel the success of "easier" short-term goals, while also making progress on longer-term goals. The overall question the workgroup wants to ask is: How can we help our program move higher on the Anti-Ism Scale?

The goals will be set by the workgroup based on the survey data, Anti-Ism Scale, and overall workgroup discussions. It is recommended to start with three goals: one short-term goal that can be completed within months, one goal that can be completed in a school year, and one goal that is longer term that may take several years to complete.

When writing the goals, it is important to make sure they are S.M.A.R.T. (specific, measurable, achievable, realistic, and time bound). The Anti-Ism Action Plan (see Figure 8.2) is available to help your team think through this process and develop an action plan.

Let us walk through how to use this action plan. First, at the top of the action plan, is "organization name." This is where you put the name of your program or organization. The next line down states "current level." This is where you write the current level on the Anti-Ism Scale that was decided for your program by the Diversity Workgroup. Stating it at the top of the action plan creates a way for you to document your program's growth.

The next and largest section of the action plan is where the workgroup sets goals. As already stated, it is recommended to have one short-term goal, one goal for a year, and one goal that may take longer (years) to complete. Once the S.M.A.R.T. goals are developed, it is time to break down the goals into workable pieces. This is much like the process of backward planning. We start with the end goal or objective and then plan backward to get to the final goal. There is no set number of action steps recommended; rather, expand or contract the action plan as your team needs.

The second column is where to document strategies that will help lead to the overall goal. The third column is the timeline column. When is the "due date" for the strategy and/or goal to be completed? In the timeline column, it is also important to add the name of the person or group of individuals who will complete the strategy. This provides a sense of accountability for the whole team. Finally, the last column is the success criteria column, which should detail what it will look like when the specific goal is met. How will the organization know when the goal is met?

To track the progress on each of the goals, it is important to revisit and discuss the action plan throughout the year. A great strategy is to discuss the goals and any progress on the strategies at each leadership meeting and/or at each Diversity Workgroup meeting.

An example, not from Program Apples, is provided in Figure 8.3. As evident in the example, selecting goals and multiple action steps to achieve the goals will help your organization accomplish the end goal of inclusion.

You may notice in Figure 8.3 that an additional column is added titled "people responsible." This was added to identify who would be the point person in charge of ensuring the work was completed, as well as reporting out to the whole group. It is your choice as a coach and/or workgroup to decide on the action plan format that works best for the needs of the program. The reason the "people responsible" column was added to this specific action plan was because many of the conversations in this program assigned the work to administration. However, it is not on the backs

Organization name:			
Current level:			
Action steps	Strategies	Timeline	Success criteria
Objective/Goal 1:			
Objective/Goal 2:			
Objective/Goal 3:			

Figure 8.2. Anti-Ism Action Plan.

Objective 1: Leadership (administration and board) develops foundational knowledge of DEIAB				
Action steps	Strategies	People responsible	Timeline	Success criteria
Approve DEI definition from DEI commission	DEI commission board members introduce and provide background on the definition	Board members of DEI commission	October 2021 Board Meeting	Accepted and approved at the board level
Attend three 1-hour sessions for DEI knowledge growth and development	Session 1: DEIAB overview Session 2: Implicit biases and microaggressions Session 3: Anti-Ism Scale and movement forward (cycle of socialization)	DEI board members and outside consultant	January—Session 1 February—Session 2 March—Session 3	All board members attend and fully participate in the trainings/workshops Provide reflections of the process at the end of the three sessions
Objective 2: Board policy and manual review				
Action steps	Strategies	People responsible	Timeline	Strategies
Review and edit, if needed, all policies	Collectively evaluate the language in the policies Suggest additional needed handbook materials Reach out to wider YMCA and community efforts	DEI committee with board approval	TBD—targeting January–June 2022	Accepted and approved at the board level

Figure 8.3. Example of goals and action steps.

of administration to ensure all the work is completed. Teachers, staff, and other personnel need to also be held accountable for the DEIAB work of the program.

Finally, if there are any disagreements among the group members along the way, it is important that the coach acts as a mediator who hears all sides and provides a final decision for the work to move forward. However, it is imperative that everyone feels as if their voice is being heard and valued in this process.

9

Program Integration

"The hardest part of any important task is getting started on it in the first place. Once you actually begin work on a valuable task, you seem to be naturally motivated to continue."

—Brian Tracy

Full program integration involves several parties, including staff, students, administration, families, and the wider school community. In this chapter, we discuss how to create an equity-focused classroom culture, which can be led by the work of the Diversity Workgroup.

PROGRAM INTEGRATION PLAN

Guided by the coach, the Diversity Workgroup must identify what is in their locus of control. What can they change within the learning environment?

CASE STUDY: PROGRAM APPLES

The Diversity Workgroup at Program Apples developed a plan for the work they wanted to complete as part of their purpose. Figure 9.1 is the working copy of their work.

Together, the Diversity Workgroup and coach discussed the current rating on the Anti-Ism Scale and solidified the work into action items (see Figure 9.1). Based on the list and brainstorming that occurred during the "Throw Me Your Idea" activity, concepts were put into action items.

> **Committee work**
> **Lesson plan (LP) template:** Include WEEKLY diversity
> - 2021–22 LP Template remote learning/diversity columns
>
> **Lesson plan activities**
> - Holidays
> - I Am/Flags/Student Month
> - Artifacts/books
>
> **Parent engagement:** Yearly plan for books and family activities
>
> **Newsletter/social media posts**
> - Develop a plan for diversity committee to send out S'more (program wide)
>   - Covers early childhood education and prevention initiative—touches overall
>   - Linking a YouTube video
>   - Family Month Activity
>   - Make a decision in August
>
> **Parent engagement**
> - Monthly take-home activities
>
> **Calendars**
> **Snack** (infused throughout)

Figure 9.1. Working copy of Diversity Workgroup plan for Program Apples.

First, the Diversity Workgroup decided to redesign their lesson plan to include embedded diversity each week. They then decided to provide guidance for lesson planning around "traditional" holidays (Halloween, Thanksgiving, Christmas, Valentine's Day, Easter, St. Patrick's Day). From their brainstorming activity, they also decided to focus on family engagement, which included many areas such as take-home activities and a class calendar. Through these activities, the goal of the Program Apple's Diversity Workgroup was to inform all stakeholders at each part of the process and provide replacement activities. Through their own learning as a Diversity Workgroup, they deeply understood the fear of "losing the known" that many of their colleagues felt. The workgroup wanted to make sure that even though something was being "taken away," there was something in its place to start new traditions and excitement in the learning environment.

Breaking down the work into subgroups, as illustrated in Figure 9.1, and providing action-oriented items, the work did not seem tedious, overwhelming, or pointless, but rather meaningful and immediately actionable.

Another item that was part of the action plan included artifacts and books selected by the Diversity Workgroup because, after learning more about hidden curriculum, the workgroup believed that was an area of growth for their program. The subcommittee (two team members) focused on the artifacts and books.

They researched and compiled a list of books that could be purchased to represent windows, mirrors, and sliding glass doors within the various classroom environments. In addition, they evaluated the artifacts in the classrooms, such as sombreros, clogs, and Chinese dragons, and began to think outside the box. They asked themselves: What is culture to the students? Are we perpetuating stereotypes through the artifacts that are included in the classroom? Through this process, they developed a list of artifacts to include in the classroom with reasoning and justification, meaning these items were not just added to fulfill the diversity quota; teachers were instructed to explain the items and incorporate them into the everyday language that is used in the classroom.

Another part of the Diversity Workgroup focused on getting information out to the wider community (i.e., families), specifically through newsletters and social media posts. This subgroup planned social media posts that corresponded to the work they were completing as a program, as well as the family activities that were planned for yearlong implementation.

Finally, the program had a long-standing process of developing a "cultural snack calendar." On this calendar, a "cultural snack" was planned for each month. The snacks included chips and salsa for Mexico, pizza for Italy, naan for India, and pretzels for Germany. All these snacks were stereotypical and, at times, Americanized concepts of food from other countries. As we have already discussed in this book, culture does not mean country. Therefore, this subgroup worked with the family activity committee to design ways for families to send in recipes (or ideas) of their favorite home snacks. This created a way to bring the culture and traditions of each family into the classroom.

INEVITABLE PROGRAM PUSHBACK

Throughout this book, we use words such as "uncomfortable" and "difficult" to describe the work of DEIAB transformation. With that being said, when it is time to focus on program integration, the inevitable pushback often begins from the wider staff population. Pushback displays fear, which sometimes leads to growth, but more often leads to tension. It is important to embrace the tension, pushback, and fear. Remember people have been socialized to have certain beliefs that have been reaffirmed by their environment. As a coach, Diversity Workgroup member, and school community member, grounding yourself in the "why" of this work is essential to keep moving toward change and transformation.

CASE STUDY: PROGRAM APPLES

At the first Diversity Workgroup–led workshop, there was a clear division between the staff members who were ready to learn and integrate DEIAB and the staff members who were 100% against this work. One staff member stated, "My White husband has lost a job to a Black man because he was Black. How is Affirmative Action and this work going to make any progress for us?" When discussing LGBTQIA+ families and representation, another member stated, "You are trying to tell us we all have to live the lifestyle of gay people. Our kids are not going to lose anything in their life because they will not be gay."

When these comments were made, the Diversity Workgroup, coaches, and administration provided support with responses such as, "We understand your questions; however, we are approaching this work through a developmentally appropriate lens, and this is something we are going to be doing programwide." Although these statements did not change the view of many of the staff members, it did make it clear that the program was moving forward with the work of inclusivity and transformation.

EDUCATING THE EDUCATOR

With the division growing among the staff members, a FAQ (Frequently Asked Questions) form was sent out, which is provided in Figure 9.2.

REFLECTION

What can you do as a coach in a situation like Program Apples? What does this specific case study tell us about the work of creating more equitable learning environments?

Q: What is the point of the diversity changes we are making in the program?
- Transforming environments to be inclusive of all identities and developing empathy for staff, families, and children.
  - (Empathy: the ability to understand and share the feelings of another.)
  - How are you showing empathy to all types of children, how they identify, and family traditions in your classroom?

Q: We can't celebrate any holidays or even talk about holidays in the school building?
- No, you are more than welcome to talk about traditions, holidays that are celebrated, and so on if guided by child interest. However, there should not be any lesson plans focused on one specific holiday. This includes no Elf on the Shelf, Easter Bunny, Santa Claus, Leprechauns, etc.

Q: Can I talk about holidays in my classroom?
- Yes, when it is child led, you are more than welcome to talk about all types of holidays and traditions that occur throughout the entire year. However, make sure to not assume, through your language, that everyone does the same thing or celebrates the same holidays.
- It is great to share your traditions and things you enjoy doing with your family or other groups of people around times of the year that you find important in your life or your children find important in their lives.

Q: You are taking away something that parents are going to be mad about. What am I supposed to do?
- Let families know we are creating a more inclusive environment, which will create a safe and welcoming place for them, as well as all of the families that enter our classroom. Although we will not celebrate holidays, such as Halloween, by putting on costumes at school or charting the types of candy gathered during trick or treating, we will be making great memories in the classroom, just like they will be creating fantastic memories at home. Those are experiences the children are more than welcome to share; however, there will be no planned lesson around any specific holiday.

Q: I still don't know what to do. What am I supposed to do?
- Read the book, *Llama, Llama Red Pajama* (YouTube search a read-aloud for *Llama, Llama Red Pajama*)
- The day of "parties," have a pajama day that includes fun activities that recap the lesson plans from the month of October.
  - May be focused around:
    - The book (*Llama, Llama Red Pajama*)
    - Fire safety: https://www.youtube.com/watch?v=s_5FqaWTj9c

Figure 9.2. Educator frequently asked questions (FAQs).

NEXT STEPS: CONTINUING TO LEARN

There are still actions steps individual educators can take to create an equity-focused classroom, such as the following:

- Change everyday language to be more gender inclusive (change "boys" and "girls" to "friends").

- Evaluate the learning environment to constantly reflect and eliminate hidden curriculum.

- Change the greetings to families on home communication; specifically, change "mom" and "dad" to "families."

In addition, there are three activities that can help in the continued learning and growth of staff members. First, the Star Activity is used to teach empathy to adults. Second, the Cycle of Socialization, accompanied by the Doll Test, is a way to ground the reasoning for the work of reflection and growth. Finally, the last activity is a Hidden Bias video that shows the Cycle of Socialization in action.

Activity to Develop Empathy

Although there are many activities to teach empathy, one we recommend is from the Trevor Project called the Star Activity. Although the goals of the Star Activity, as described on the Trevor Project website, are to describe the aspects and feelings of "coming out," we often use this activity to help participants understand empathy. The Trevor Project (n.d.) explained that this activity "examine[s] our judgements of others in a safe and productive way and explore the importance of self-identification" (para. 1).

In the Star Activity, each participant is provided with an "identity" based on the color of star they receive (red, blue, purple, or orange). The participants are instructed to place a specific word on each of the five points of the star. Point 1 is the name of a very close friend. Point 2 is a community that is important to you, such as a profession, religious organization, or group of friends. Point 3 is a family member you go to for advice—someone in your family you trust fully. Point 4 is your dream job. And, finally, Point 5 is a hope or dream.

Once each of the five points are filled out, each color star is instructed to either tear or bend a point, which is to represent losing permanently or temporarily something important to them based on their identity. By the end of the activity, each color star has had a different experience because of who and what they have "lost" in the activity. This is supposed to simulate being ostracized based on marginality. Although the Star Activity is on a website that supports the LGBTQIA+ community, it is not an activity based on "being gay," but rather what it feels like to lose people or things purely based on your identity.

> **REFLECTION**
>
> How can the Star Activity add to your own growth journey in regard to empathy for oppressed groups? If you are part of an oppressed group, what might you add to this activity?

Cycle of Socialization

After the opening Star Activity, it is time to reflect on the Cycle of Socialization (see Figure 9.3), which helps us understand how the socialization patterns each of us experienced play a multitude of direct roles in our lives. Our socialization patterns influence how we are impacted by issues of oppression and how we help maintain an oppressive system based on power.

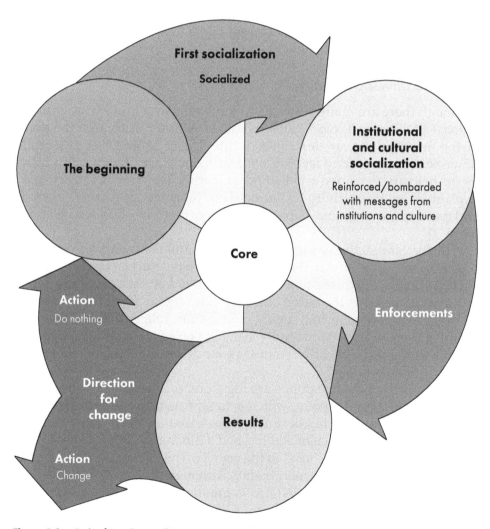

Figure 9.3. Cycle of Socialization. (*Source:* Harro, 1997.)

In this cycle, it is evident that the core of our socialization is led by fear, ignorance, confusion, and/or insecurity. These concepts can result in either stagnation, which would continue the cycle of bias, or change to interrupt the status quo. We have the choice to continue the stagnation of oppressive thoughts, actions, and environments, or we can decide to change to create an equitable and safe space for all individuals. The outside of the cycle consists of three circles starting at the beginning, moving to institutions and culture, and ending with the result.

The first circle represents the beginning of our life. What were you born into? In the beginning, we do not have control over the messages we receive or the people we are around. We are either born into privilege or not, which is often accompanied by racial profiling, lack of power, and discrimination.

Furthermore, as soon as we are born, we are embedded in the socialization process, which is represented by the first (top) arrow. Are we given a pink blanket or a blue blanket? Are we given White baby dolls, Black baby dolls, or no baby dolls—only trucks? Are we allowed to wear a dress or not allowed to wear a dress? Do we hear positive words regarding differences or negative words regarding differences? What are the subtle or not-so-subtle rules of gender, race, and other identities that are being communicated in the first years of socialization? What we learn in our first experiences with socialization is our family or community view of "right" or "good" and "wrong" or "bad." Will we have consequences if we rebel and/or be praised if we conform?

In the Cycle of Socialization, Upchurch (2021) explained, "the second circle represents the institutions that help shape our views and beliefs, and help instill within us prejudice or acceptance" (para. 5). How do the institution and history of medicine affect us if we decide to go to the doctor when we are sick? How do the institution and history of education affect us if we have positive or negative experiences? How do media, song lyrics, or the practices of the legal system affect our view of the world, our implicit biases, and our prejudices for or against a group of people or institution? How do social media and what peers or acquaintances post affect our views, experiences, and socialization?

Extending from the second circle is the second arrow. This represents how ideas, beliefs, and behaviors are instilled into the systems and into our thought processes. These are the concepts of institutional and structural racism, gender dynamics in the workplace, and overall complacency.

As is illustrated in the Cycle of Socialization, going against the status quo is not easy because we are rewarded for doing "good," according to the Eurocentric view of good, and punished for being bad, or going against the Eurocentric view by rebelling or questioning oppressive societal norms.

The third and final circle in the cycle represents what Upchurch (2021) described as "the devastating result upon all of us that this self-perpetuated cycle of oppression produces" (para. 7). We internalize and act on the oppressive ideologies of silence, dehumanization, and power. Stemming from this final circle, we have a choice. We have the choice to do nothing and continue to perpetuate the cycle of oppression, or we can do something, speak out, learn, reflect, and push against the oppression in our society.

> **REFLECTION**
>
> Take time to reflect on each part of the Cycle of Socialization in regard to your life. If you would like to watch a YouTube video to help process the cycle, please see the video "Social Conditioning" posted on August 13, 2018, by Diverse City LLC (https://www.youtube.com/watch?v=mPp7uaGYdDw). In your reflection, share how this connects to your work in the early childhood education field.

When we introduce the Cycle of Socialization in workshops, we follow by introducing the Doll Test Study, which is a famous study conducted by psychologists Kenneth and Mamie Clark in the 1940s. The Doll Test Study shows the psychological impacts of segregation on all children, including Black children. As stated by the NAACP Legal Defense and Education Fund (2019):

> Drs. Clark used four dolls, identical except for color, to test children's racial perceptions. Their subjects, children between the ages of three to seven, were asked to identify both the race of the dolls and which color doll they prefer. A majority of the children preferred the White doll and assigned positive characteristics to it. The Clarks concluded that "prejudice, discrimination, and segregation" created a feeling of inferiority among African-American children and damaged their self-esteem." (para. 2)

This study has been repeated multiple times since the 1940s with the same results. (The video we often show is titled "Doll Test: The Effects of Racism on Children [ENG]" posted on YouTube by Fanpage.it [https://www.youtube.com/watch?v=QRZPw-9sJtQ].)

The Cycle of Socialization, paired with the Doll Test information (and YouTube video), provides a basis for understanding how implicit biases are innate, but we can actively work against the cycle to be on the trajectory of change.

> **REFLECTION**
>
> How do the Cycle of Socialization and the Doll Test affect your work as an early childhood coach? How will you guide teachers to understand the impact of these two activities in their work as early childhood educators?

Hidden Bias

At the conclusion of this series of learning, we often circle back to the first concept of empathy and experiencing marginalization. We combine all the information by showing a culminating video about hidden bias.

The specific video we show is called "Our Hidden Biases" (Picture Alternatives, 2019). The video walks through the life of a Black boy from the time he was about preschool age until he is a teenager. It shows his life experiences where he continually faces hidden biases throughout his life. At the end of the 4:44-minute video, it shows an experience in an early childhood classroom that fully displays the marginalization the Black male has learned, as well as the learned concept of power and privilege for a White male student. The video ends with two questions:

- Do you see yourself in this story?
- How does your bias impact others?

Another topic within the hidden bias video that you can engage colleagues in discussing focuses on the first 2:38 minutes. The first part of the video specifically focuses on the interactions a family experiences day in and day out within their community.

> **REFLECTION**
>
> If a family is coming to your program that is constantly experiencing microaggressions within their community, what might their engagement strategies or attitude be regarding an early childhood education setting? How will you, as an educator, provide a welcoming environment that does not continue the microaggressions they experience on a daily basis?

You can also invite participants to watch the video several times with a different lens, and we promise they (and you) will see additional concepts each time.

AFFINITY GROUPS

"The affinity space was a place of affirmation and empowerment that we all so desperately needed. We acknowledged shared experiences in ways that were productive, valuable, and meaningful. It was a brave space that preserved our dignity as a people."
—Trina Moore-Southall

Affinity groups are controversial; however, we highly recommend using them as a way to speak more in the "we."

We have experience with embedding and not embedding affinity groups into our workshops. Overwhelmingly, the individuals who self-identify as Black and Brown on the postworkshop surveys indicate the need for affinity groups. Specifically, in one training that did not include affinity groups, one participant who identified as Black commented that some of the videos focus specifically on race and should be optional for Black and Brown participants since many of the topics are part of their lived experience. Providing an optional breakout room and including affinity groups are essential for reaching all participants. This participant went on to state, "If you claim that white folx learning shouldn't be on the backs of our BIPOC colleagues you need to back that up with your actions."

During the affinity sessions, which are often facilitated by peers (but guided by the professional development providers), we often split the group into a self-identified White group and a self-identified group of BIPOC+. However, there are multiple ways you can divide the group based on oppressed and privileged identities, such as a right-handed group and a left-handed group, with the knowledge that the world is predominately created for right-handed individuals. Another example is to divide groups by Christian and non-Christian, with the knowledge that most societal institutions ascribe to Christian-based holidays and teachings. Regardless of the groups for this activity, the key is to divide based on historically perceived binary identities, one of privilege and one of oppression.

If you choose a right-handed and left-handed affinity group, write down everything that is "made" with you in mind. Once these are reflected upon, discuss how this makes moving through life "easy" or "hard." If you are right-handed, think about it: The way a computer mouse is set up is based on right-handedness, most scissors are for right-handed people, gearshifts in American cars are on the right side, and the list goes on. As a right-handed parent of three left-handed children, I (Reinking) know that to find a video on tying shoes left-handed is sometimes difficult without adding the descriptor "left-handed." Our world is made for people who are right-handed.

In workshops we lead, we will often divide the group based on race. Dr. Reinking, the White member of the training duo, begins the White affinity group with this statement, "Many of you want to know what is happening in the group for Black, indigenous, and people of color, also referred to BIPOC+. That is not our business; however, it shows the privilege we have experienced our entire lives of expecting we, as White people, to be welcomed in all environments. That is not the case. We are here in our group and will be learning in our group with each other."

One time when this statement was shared, a participant unmuted and said, "That reminds me of college. I heard of the Black prom that was happening, and I tried to talk my friends into inviting me because I wanted to see what was happening. I never got invited, but I realized it was not a place for me to be nosey, but rather a place for them to connect without White people always taking over."

Mrs. Thigpen, the Black member of the training duo, begins her affinity group explaining the self-selection for people of the BIPOC+ group was created to provide a space for Black and Brown teachers to discuss the realities of being a teacher. Through the affinity group, the educators are able to see themselves represented through the presentation materials, share their own experiences, and connect with other Black and Brown educators within their organization. When the BIPOC+ affinity group begins, Mrs. Thigpen states that the purpose of this affinity group is to provide a safe space for us, as BIPOC+ educators.

Overall, the affinity groups provide a sense of belonging, as well a safe space for individuals to have in-depth discussions. If most staff members do not want to engage in affinity groups outside of the professional learning session, offer other resources to staff who may want to continue the discussion. There are multiple groups in many communities around the United States that create a safe space for individuals to learn, grow, and discuss. For example, GLSEN (Gay, Lesbian & Straight Education Network), SURJ (Showing Up for Racial Justice), NAACP (National Association for the Advancement of Colored People), and NCFA (National Council for Adoption).

BOOK STUDIES

Another way to continue the learning throughout the year is to arrange book study groups (not based in affinity group identities). Book studies are a way to engage all members of the community in further self-discovery and learning. When choosing books, it is important to look for books that discuss equity, social justice, or diversity. At first, the book does not need to be education focused but can be focused on overall bias and microaggressions. As the book studies continue, it is important to transition from overarching equity work to specifically education-related equity work. Finally, when finding a book, make sure the author either identifies as part of the in-group discussed in the book or has a proven record (conduct a search on the Internet) of equity-focused work through an asset-based (not deficit-based) mindset.

The case study we have been following, Program Apples, engaged in book studies for 1 year at the beginning of their work toward programmatic changes.

CASE STUDY: PROGRAM APPLES

When asked to work with Program Apples, the curriculum coach knew there would be a big learning curve for many of the staff members. Therefore, we suggested engaging in the low-level, low-threat activity of book groups that are accompanied by discussions and learning activities. The two books the group of teachers read over the course of the school year were *Multicultural Teaching in the Early Childhood Classroom* by Mariana Souto-Manning (2013) and *Leading Anti-Bias Early Childhood Programs* by Louise Derman-Sparks, Debbie LeeKeenan, and John Nimmo (2015). Through these book studies, the teachers were guided through discussion of the four goals of antibias education (i.e., the zones of change: comfort, fear, learning, and growth), defining what diversity is and is not, and questions that are asked throughout the two books.

10

Structural (Transformative) Change

*"The greatest danger in times of turbulence is not the turbulence;
it is to act with yesterday's logic."*
—Peter Drucker

Our goal is transformation. When you refer back to the Anti-Ism Scale, transformation is at the highest level. However, to change a structure, you have to start with the foundation. By this part in the book, you may have identified program policies that need to be revised, practices that need to be changed, and perhaps specific areas of growth for the wider program staff. Identifying all of these pieces is just another part of your journey to structural change.

MULTICULTURAL CURRICULUM IMPLEMENTATION

Specific to structural change is the implementation of multicultural curriculum at the classroom level. Great Schools Partnership (2013a) defined multicultural curriculum as "any form of education or teaching that incorporates the histories, texts, values, beliefs, and perspectives of people from different cultural backgrounds" (para. 1). Therefore, we must acknowledge the reality that the classroom curriculum was developed by publishers that do not know the specific demographics of your classroom. When thinking about how to incorporate multicultural education into your existing curriculum, there are five stages developed by Banks (1999) and added to by McIntosh (2000) to consider:

1. Curriculum of the Mainstream
2. Contributions Approach (Heroes and Holidays)
3. Additive Approach (Integration Stage)
4. Transformation Approach (Structural Reform Stage)
5. Social Action Approach (Multicultural, Social Action, and Awareness Stage)

In the Curriculum of the Mainstream approach, the information is presented in a Eurocentric manner, or a manner that focuses on the White majority view and mindset of topics. Essentially, this is the traditional method of education due to the institutional and structural racism present in the education system. An example of this level would include a lesson only about the Pilgrims at Thanksgiving or predominately about White peoples' influences in and perspectives of society through the years.

The Contributions Approach, which is also known as the Heroes and Holidays approach, is an approach where perspectives outside of the majority view are only given when the individual is a hero, such as Martin Luther King, Jr.; Cesare Chavez; or Rosa Parks. Or it is around a holiday when "othering" can be brought into the classroom, such as Kwanzaa or Hanukkah before the winter holiday in December, while also predominantly incorporating Christmas traditions. Essentially, in this stage, teachers incorporate books and activities to celebrate the "heroes and holidays" during specific times of the year.

In the Additive Approach or Integration Stage, teachers begin to integrate content, concepts, themes, and perspectives to the already established curriculum without changing the basic structure (Banks, 1999). Teachers who incorporate this stage of multicultural curriculum take an already existing unit and add in diversity. For example, a unit on transportation would incorporate pictures of people of various genders operating vehicles, along with people of various races and abilities. Another example would be a teacher including male nurses and Black female doctors during a unit on professions or community helpers. Essentially, the unit title does not change, but the depictions of various individuals are added to the already existing unit.

In the Transformation Approach or Structural Reform Stage, teachers change the curricular structure in the classroom to encourage students to view concepts, issues, themes, and problems from several cultural perspectives. An example of this approach would be to teach students about the Native American perspective and Pilgrim perspective around the time of Thanksgiving. Another would be to understand the multiple perspectives of the story behind Christopher Columbus, rather than only the White, male, dominant perspective. Although those are just two prominent examples, the idea of the Transformation Approach is that all lessons are transformed to see multiple perspectives throughout the school year and not only for "heroes and holidays."

Finally, the Social Action Approach, or the Multicultural, Social Action, and Awareness Stage, in essence, adds to the changes made in Stage 4 but also encourages students to question and act on social issues (Banks, 1999; McIntosh, 2000). Examples of this in an early childhood classroom might include writing to a large chain grocery store to persuade the executives to build a grocery store in a food desert in their community or to make blankets for veterans and/or homeless in their community. The goal of this stage is for students to see all of the perspectives and know that their voice and actions can make a change in their community and the wider world. Essentially, in this stage, students and teachers engage in social action with community members.

> **REFLECTION**
>
> What is your current level of multicultural curriculum implementation in your learning environment? Support your reflection with specific examples and engage in wider discussions with fellow educators in your program regarding the specific examples.

Another way to evaluate the multicultural education within your classroom is to use Nieto's (1994) levels of multicultural education support. Next are definitions of each of Nieto's levels: Monocultural, tolerance, acceptance, and respect.

1. *Monocultural:* A situation in which school structures, policies, curricula, instructional materials, and even pedagogical strategies are primarily representative of only the dominant culture. This level is exclusionary and often does not include representation from historically oppressed identities. The mirrors, windows, and sliding glass doors for the diverse student population are not presented.

2. *Tolerance:* To tolerate differences means that they are endured, not necessarily embraced. This level of support for multicultural education stands on shaky ground because what is tolerated today can easily be rejected tomorrow. This level does not present a space for students and staff to be their authentic selves.

3. *Acceptance:* Differences are acknowledged, and their importance is neither denied nor belittled. At this level, schoolteachers discuss differences and learn not to be blind to others' identities.

4. *Respect:* Admiration and high esteem for differences. At this level, the diverse teaching staff embeds multicultural education into the entire school system, ranging from classroom content to school culture.

> **REFLECTION**
>
> Just as you did before, reflect on your current level of multicultural curriculum implementation in your learning environment based on Nieto's (2008) work. Support your reflection with specific examples and engage in wider discussions with fellow educators in your program regarding the specific examples.

TRANSFORMATIVE OR STRUCTURAL CHANGE

As evident from the evaluation of multicultural classroom curriculum, transformative or structural change is at the core of this work but is not easy to implement. Coaches and supervisors and the wider Diversity Workgroup can implement structural change by guiding educators in delivery, content, and materials. In simple terms, implementing multicultural education is based on empathy and fairness, something that is easily implemented in early childhood classrooms. According to Derman-Sparks et al.:

> This goal [the antibias education goal of justice] is about building children's innate, budding capacities for empathy and fairness as well as their cognitive skills for thinking critically about what is happening around them. It is about building a sense of safety—the sense that everyone can and will be treated fairly. (2020, p. 16)

So, how do we truly implement multicultural education through delivery, specific content, and materials? Delivery spans from instructional techniques to understanding power dynamics. It is important to vary instructional techniques throughout the year, such as cooperative learning, small-group discussion, and individual learning. As part of delivery, it is important to understand the dynamics of power in the room so you do not perpetuate privilege and oppression. Therefore, being intentional to respect and value everyone in the room, no matter their identity, is key.

Moving from delivery to content, it is vital to ensure the information that is being taught is accurate, truthful, and developmentally appropriate. However, it is hard to ask teachers to teach truth when the provided curriculum often includes one-sided history accounts filled with Christian and Eurocentric views. This may mean that educators need to bring in ideas most curriculum developers (and, truthfully, schools) do not include in mainstream education. As a reminder, the backlash to critical race theory is purely a backlash to teaching true American history.

In addition, study the history of discrimination in curriculum and ensure that you are not replicating it. Educating yourself on the history of discrimination of different groups of people provides you with a lens to see the injustices that are present in people's lives.

Arguably, varying instructional techniques (delivery) is just as important as varying instructional materials. To provide varying materials and techniques, teachers need to be cognizant of their materials and practices by:

- Examining all materials for bias and oppressive content by checking for stereotypes and inaccurate images.

- Diversifying images and content throughout the entire year, not only during specific months or celebrations.

- Presenting content from a variety of perspectives and angles.

- Presenting content through a variety of lenses, not just the heroic characters.

- Bringing the perspectives and experiences of the students into the learning experience, which will increase student engagement. (This means you have to learn the identities of your children.)

- Encouraging students to ask critical questions about all information they receive from you and curricular materials and modeling this type of critical thinking for them. (In early childhood education, an example would be a teacher presenting a book to the students and having them look at the cover and asking them, "Why do you think we are reading this book?" Another example is when a teacher presents information and asks the students, "How do you know this?" and allows the students to justify or present their reasoning for their answer to the question.)

- Making content and delivery relevant for the students, which means facilitating experiences in which they connect what they are learning to their everyday lives.

- Recognizing students as the most important multicultural resource. Your students bring a great wealth of knowledge; it is your job to see it.

- Incorporating discussions about difference and inequality into their lessons. For example, looking at the playgrounds and buildings and seeing if they are wheelchair accessible allows teachers and students to have conversations on inequality.

- Providing names and stories of other people who have fought social injustices, such as Harvey Milk, John Lewis, Madonna Thunder Hawk, and Brittney Packnett Cunningham.

- Honestly discussing the history of privilege and oppression in subject areas, school, education, and society at large in a developmentally appropriate way.

- Connecting teaching and learning to local community issues and larger global issues.

- Encouraging students to think critically about the United States, capitalism, the two-party system, and other traditionally untouchable subjects of critique.

- Working with professional learning communities or a team of teachers to examine and provide feedback on each other's curricular units, lesson plans, and entire frameworks.

- Requesting and openly accepting feedback from students and families.

- Continuing to assess practices to ensure they are still providing an equitable environment for all.

> **REFLECTION**
>
> After reading through the list, which of the practices are you currently doing? What do you plan to do within the next year? What do you plan to implement as your longer-term goals based on this list?

CASE STUDY: PROGRAM APPLES

Program Apples identified the Additive Approach multicultural curriculum level when analyzing the classroom curriculum and implementation across their program. This was based on the realization that the curriculum had not been transformed over the past 10 years, but rather, information and ideas were being added with metaphorical scotch tape and pencil markings that could be erased. This hodgepodge of curriculum had the intent of leaving traditions (or "we have always done this" activities) intact, while also attempting to transform to a culturally responsive curriculum.

Realizing and identifying the program's level of the Additive Approach, the Diversity Workgroup spent much of their planning time preparing for the implementation process to make the structural change easier for their colleagues. As part of that process, they developed several programwide implementation plans. One activity was the development of a more inclusive Family Flag activity.

The Family Flag activity (see Figure 10.1) has been in the program for at least a decade; however, it was always implemented during the first month of school and rarely visited again. Through the planning process with the Diversity Workgroup, it was decided to implement the Family Flag to be more purposeful, identity based, and implemented every month. The plan they created was provided to all teachers. This is just one of the items that was planned for ease of implementation by the Diversity Workgroup.

Another item was the family home activities. The goal of this activity was to engage families in exploring their traditions, cultures, and communities. The idea is that when children and families complete the take-home activity, it will be added to a Family Flag book that can then be sent home at the end of the school year. This book will provide insight into the work the family did (or the child did in class if it is not completed at home), and it is also a way to show the child's progression in the academic domains of literacy and writing.

> **Monthly Family Flag/("This Is Me Book") and "I am _____"**
>
> **August:** Traditional Family Flag as given during orientation/home visits
> "I am (3, 4, 5) years old; my birthday is _____."
>
> **September:** Who makes up this family? Who are my family members?
> (siblings/fosters/grandparents/aunties, uncles/neighbors)
> Helper jobs/roles in the classroom
> "I am a (helper/son/daughter/cousin/nephew)."
>
> **October:** My family home/we are safe
> "I am safe because: we practice fire safety; we wear seatbelts; we attend wellness checkups."
>
> **November:** Family foods/dishes that we enjoy/recipes
> "I am grateful for _____ foods."
>
> **December:** What days/events are special for your family? Reunions? Gotcha day? Festivals/traditions?
>
> **January:** What talents/skills/job trades does your family have? What goals do they have? What do you want to be when you grow up?
> "I am (brave; a dancer; a builder; a painter; a poet; a musician)."
>
> **February:** Ways your family shows kindness/love/support/compassion
> "I am a friend/companion because _____."
>
> **March:** Our family enjoys making art together/recreation/games/hobbies; Youth Art Month
> "I am an artist because _____. I am active because _____."
>
> **April:** How does your family enjoy nature or take care of the earth? Spring changes/Earth Day
> "I am (a keeper of the earth, recycler, naturalist, bug-keeper)."
>
> **May:** Our family is creative (gardening, planting seeds, bubbles, sidewalk chalk)
> "I am creative _____."

Figure 10.1. Family Flag activity.

A more descriptive explanation of the Family Flag activity used in Program Apples is that families were provided a prompt each month to complete with their child at home and then send into the classroom. The monthly activity was hung on the wall, in the same place the long-standing Family Flags were hung previously. When the month ended and a new activity was sent home, the previous activities were bound together in a book for each student to take home at the end of year. In addition, throughout the year, the books were kept in the classroom for students to read about themselves or learn about each other. Overall, the revised Family Flag activity was designed to provide a home–school connection as a way to create a welcoming environment.

In addition to the new Family Flag activity, more family activities were sent home that were connected to the monthly theme as well as the Family Flag activity. The specific family take-home projects designed by the Diversity Workgroup included the following:

- *August:* At the beginning of the year home visit, the teachers will discuss the Family Flag activity and explain the way it will be implemented all year long.

- *September:* Complete the All About Me activity, which includes age, family members, favorite color, and favorite food.
- *October:* Draw a simple map of your house and plan for fire safety. Where will you meet as a family? Discuss and hang the fire plan in your home.
- *November:* Each family will receive a paper plate for students to return once a favorite family recipe is written on the plate. The recipes will be made by the class, if able, throughout the months of November and December.
- *December:* Send home small swatches of fabric for families to make small tie blankets. Attached to the fabric will be winter and weather safety concepts for staying warm.
- *January:* Read the book *Snowballs* by Lois Ehlert. Send home a white piece of paper and instruct families to make snow people.
- *February:* Send home a postcard with the instructions to write a letter to a favorite person or family member. Provide the opportunity for students to bring the postcard back to school and mail it.
- *March:* Send home watercolors and skin tone crayons. Encourage the families to draw, color, and paint pictures of their spring environment.
- *April:* Send contact paper home with the instructions to go on an art nature walk. While walking around outside, in your community or in another area, pick up pieces of nature that represent different colors of the rainbow. (Do not pick up trash as part of this project unless deemed safe by the family.)
- *May:* Send home instructions on how to make instruments with items around your house. Also send home small objects that can be added to the home instruments.

OUTSIDE THE CLASSROOM

The work of transformation does not happen in a learning environment bubble but expands beyond the four walls of the classroom into school policies that affect staff and families, hiring practices, and language in internal and external documentation or marketing materials.

School Policies

For true multicultural education to work, the entire school system has to commit to it because wider school policies and practices affect students and families. For example, practices that police the appearance of students and punish them for wearing their hair in particular styles are discriminatory. Legislation such as the CROWN Act, which stands for Creating a Respectful and Open World for Natural Hair, led by the CROWN Coalition (2019), "prohibits race-based hair discrimination, which is the denial of employment and educational opportunities because of hair texture or protective hairstyles including braids, locs, twists or bantu knots" (para. 2). Furthermore, schools and communities around the country have advocated to ban critical race theory and some books. In the Preface, we discuss the purpose of critical race theory, which is to critically analyze structural and institutional racism to provide guidance for transformation that creates equity. If we truly desire equity for all, then we cannot ignore the systems that prevent equity from happening, such as banning teaching American history or banning books that teach students about the truth of our country.

In addition, disciplinary policies, such as zero-tolerance policies and antibullying policies, are often used to punish students when they break a rule. These policies often discriminate against certain groups of people, specifically Black and Brown students. Black students are four times more likely to be suspended than White students. Students with disabilities are twice as likely to be suspended as those without disabilities.

Another issue is that these policies do not allow for a strength-based mindset. The student who breaks a rule or is caught bullying a student continues to get more severely punished with each incident. The student is seen or labeled as a "bad student." The issue is that this policy does not allow space for teaching and educating the children through the practice of restorative justice (Gjelten, 2019). Furthermore, teachers are experiencing even more challenging behavior due to the traumatic experiences and lack of community support due to the coronavirus disease 2019 (COVID-19) pandemic. Teachers have witnessed students who have to relearn how to socialize with their peers (Belsha, 2021), who have unstructured and unstable environments, and who are disconnected from support systems. Overall, policies like these often overlook the opportunity to teach a student what appropriate behavior looks like instead of labeling them due to their behavior.

Diversity Among Staff

The commitment to multicultural education must also happen at the administration level, including hiring practices that are inclusive. To truly have a diverse teaching population, a program needs to evaluate where they are recruiting and how they are recruiting and use established programs, such as Grow-Your-Own (GYO) (Regional Educational Laboratory Southwest, 2019). GYO programs develop a partnership among state education organizations, school districts, and teacher preparation programs. The focus of these programs is to recruit young people to work in schools in their own communities. Thinking outside of the box when it comes to marketing for teacher positions will increase your chance of hiring and employing qualified and diverse populations.

Adding to the diverse teaching population, a program must also commit to having a diverse board of directors. Remember, we all see the world through our own lens. The more diverse the leadership, the more diverse perspectives are being included in decision-making processes.

> **REFLECTION**
>
> What policies, practices, and procedures in your program uplift individuals? What needs to be changed to transform policies, practices, and procedures?

External Marketing and Communication

Finally, how your program is marketed through external marketing and communications in the wider community provides insight on inclusion or exclusion practices. External communications include flyers, marketing materials, and the information the community sees about your program. It is important to evaluate your website, social media, logo, and mailings with a critical lens to decide how your organization is being portrayed to the wider community. Just as with other pieces of this work, it is important to include a variety of voices to understand the unintended impact various external communications may have on diverse identities.

CASE STUDY: PROGRAM APPLES

Part of the coaching process with Program Apples included evaluating the website and other external communications. When we critically analyzed the website, we noticed there were no Black or Brown children represented, which is also known as a visual microaggression. Therefore, the website was unintentionally stating that the program was only designed for White children and White families. When the administration was made aware of this, through reflection, they were able to immediately change the visual microaggressions being portrayed through the communication on their website.

As external coaches, we note this example as illustrating the importance of including a variety of voices at the table. When the staff is diverse and a brave space has been created, voices are no longer silenced and can truly affect structural change because this change requires many diverse voices.

11

Implications for Wider Change

*"This will never work with our population.
You are erasing who we are in this community."*

*"I am not going to take away what our community values.
This is not how we are going to move forward."*

*"This is all just part of the liberal agenda.
We are not allowing that in our community."*

*"You mean I am less than everyone else,
so you are going to take away our holidays?"*

*"So, you are asking us to change our lifestyles and preach being gay?
That is not happening. Being gay is a sin."*

In other chapters, you may have noticed quotes were added at the beginning to prime you, as the reader, to concepts that were going to be discussed. This chapter is the same; however, the above quotes are actual quotes stated during a meeting of school administrators (superintendents) when introduced to the topic of implementing DEIAB in their schools. As is obvious from these quotes, a lot of work is needed at all levels for full program integration.

Unfortunately, this is where one of the programs we were working with stalled abruptly in their implementation process. To address the stalled work, we developed two letters (Figure 11.1 and Figure 11.2) to communicate the information regarding the work.

> **REFLECTION**
>
> After reading the family letter (Figure 11.1), how might families in your program react? How will you, as the coach, guide the future work with families? With staff? In this reflection, use the information you have learned throughout this book to guide your future work with families.

> **REFLECTION**
>
> After reading the administrator letter (Figure 11.2), how might administrators in your program react? How will you, as the coach, guide the future work of the program? In this reflection, use the information you have learned throughout this book to guide your work with administrators.

Dear Families,

First, thank you for being part of our ever-growing Program Apples family. We have some exciting new activities coming this year that are aimed at creating an even more welcoming environment for you and your child(ren).

Beginning last school year, our staff began the process of learning about diversity and equity, with the goal of ensuring all our families feel welcomed, regardless of their identity. This past summer, a group of staff members worked hard on creating a roadmap for implementing the learning we did as a program. As part of that, we developed a diversity mission statement.

The diversity statement created by this group that represents our mission at Program Apples is:

> *Program Apples is a community-based program that accepts and celebrates all educators, families, caregivers, and children regardless of their identity. As a program, we are committed to creating an environment where everyone feels a sense of belonging, everyone feels empowered to grow and learn, and everyone is welcomed. Overall, our goal is to implement impactful change focused on antibias education.*

Help us enjoy some new monthly celebrations as we move away from some of the typical celebrations that do not match the mission of antibias curriculum! What does this mean for you, your family, and your child(ren)? Fun, engagement, and growth together.

- Monthly take-home activities focused on your family and child
- Developing an "I Am" book throughout the whole school year
- Fun activities in the classroom most months
  - October: Fire safety and keeping our bodies healthy at nighttime. We will be ending the month with a pajama party.
  - November: We will be focusing on nutrition, ending with a nutritious meal.
  - December: Our focus will be on favorite family recipes, ending with a cookbook.

Our goal is to develop empathy, create welcoming environments for all children and families, and build new sentimental moments for families around what role school plays in and out of their family traditions. Although we still highly encourage families and students to talk about family traditions (we even have a whole month dedicated to family traditions), our focus will be primarily on creating equity in the classroom based on our mission statement.

Figure 11.1. Family letter.

> Dear Administrators,
>
> First, I hope the start to your school year is going well. I wanted to reach out to you regarding a project we launched last year through professional development with our staff at Program Apples and that we are continuing to implement. The project focuses on transforming our classrooms to be more inclusive of all identities, regardless of family demographics or child identity. In an effort to continue our push for more equitable practices, we developed a Diversity Committee that met over the summer to plan for inclusive implementation in the upcoming school year.
>
> The diversity statement created by this group that represents our mission at Program Apples is:
>
> > *Program Apples is a community-based program that accepts and celebrates all educators, families, caregivers, and children regardless of their identity. As a program, we are committed to creating an environment where everyone feels a sense of belonging, everyone feels empowered to grow and learn, and everyone is welcomed. Overall, our goal is to implement impactful change focused on antibias education.*
>
> What does this mean for classroom(s) in your building(s)?
>
> The biggest change will be the inclusive ways we engage with families and students. Specifically, during the month of October, we will be focusing on fire safety and keeping our bodies healthy at nighttime. We will be ending the month with a pajama party as a culminating activity for our children. In November, we will be focusing on nutrition, ending with a nutritious meal, and in December, our focus will be on favorite family recipes, ending with a cookbook.
>
> Our goal is to develop empathy, create welcoming environments for all children and families, and build new sentimental moments for families around what role school plays in and out of their family traditions. Although we still highly encourage families and students to talk about family traditions (we even have a whole month dedicated to family traditions), our focus will be primarily on creating equity in the classroom based on our mission statement.
>
> In addition, we are continuing the process of learning and growing around the culturally responsive practices (and standards) in the state, which is also grounding our work.

Figure 11.2. Administrator letter.

COMMUNITY MAPPING: STRENGTHS, WEAKNESSES, OPPORTUNITIES, AND THREATS

Regardless of your program and community, it is important to complete a community map because the community you live in and the overall values and beliefs of the community will provide a certain level of influence in how families receive possible changes toward DEIAB. An easy way to complete a community map is by using a strengths, weaknesses, opportunities, and threats (SWOT) evaluation of a community. As with all of the other work introduced regarding DEIAB, make sure that a variety of voices are included when analyzing the community.

The SWOT community evaluation can be completed in collaboration with any of the activities described in this book or completely independently. Although SWOT evaluations are often used in the business field, they can also be applied to the education field.

- What are the strengths of the community? Are there nearby parks, grocery stores to walk to, libraries to access, and social services agencies to provide support?

- What are the weaknesses or barriers of the community? Is there a lack of safe outdoor space? Is there a lack of fresh food within walking distance (food desert)? Is there a lack of bus routes or are there unsafe living conditions as deemed by the state? It is important to remember that what is "safe" to one cultural identity may not be the same definition for another cultural identity. Essentially, it is important to reflect on your own background when making judgements regarding what is considered a "weakness."

- What are opportunities? What are opportunities for partnerships? Is there a library nearby so that you could invite the librarian to school or take field trips to the library? Is there an opportunity to have other walking field trips to local businesses and/or restaurants? Is there a strong sense of community (bond)?

- What are the threats? Specifically, in the context of the early childhood education environment, threats that may affect the classroom include poverty, domestic abuse, lack of a clear social service structure, and limited community support for students (e.g., no snack packs provided to students who need food over the weekend or holidays).

Regardless of the poverty rate, crime rate, school retention score, and population, every community has positives and opportunities to contribute to the well-being of the students. I (Thigpen) once worked at a center that was close to several abandoned buildings. Viewing this neighborhood from an asset mindset, I was able to use the buildings to teach my students about how buildings are built and structural strength. We were able to walk to the buildings and safely look inside to describe and discuss the internal structures.

Think about the community in which your organization is located and complete the SWOT chart shown in Figure 11.3.

Strengths of the community	Weaknesses or barriers in the community
Opportunities in the community	Threats in the community

Figure 11.3. SWOT (strengths, weaknesses, opportunities, and threats) chart of a school community.

> **REFLECTION**
>
> Reflect on your community and fill out the chart in Figure 11.3. After filling out the chart, discuss the boxes that have the most and the fewest items. Are there more barriers than opportunities? Are there more threats than strengths? If so, go back and continue to evaluate your community from an asset-based mindset.

Completing the SWOT chart is one more way for staff members to begin to think differently about the school and wider community. By understanding the various aspects of the school and community, staff members can more fully advocate for the work of including equity, specifically windows, mirrors, and sliding glass doors, into the learning environments.

As stated previously, not everyone wants this work to take place. Some will be more hesitant to implement changes based on certain identities. This can be disheartening, especially when those who are in positions of power and influence do not see the value in making transformative changes. Although some programs stall their DEIAB transformative work based on tension-filled divisions between staff members, it is only stalled. The individual work can continue.

For example, Program Apples ebbed and flowed between moving forward and stalling throughout the years. However, during the stalled periods, some staff members continued individual and group work that influenced the overall program and classroom in transformative practices.

ILLINOIS CASE STUDY

Knowing the laws and mandates of your state is important for DEIAB work. Does your state ban books based on critical race theory (CRT) justifications? Is there information that explicitly calls out CRT in standards or policies? Does your state explicitly state the type of history that needs to be taught in schools? Overall, it is important to know where your state stands in regard to equity-focused teaching and learning in prekindergarten to Grade 12 classrooms.

In the state of Illinois, there are numerous mandates within Illinois code that explicitly state that historically marginalized identities need to be included into curriculum. For example, House Bill 246 was signed into law in 2019 and stated, "In public schools only, the teaching of history shall include a study of the roles and contributions of lesbian, gay, bisexual, and transgender people in the history of this country and this State" (as cited in Jackson, 2019, para. 3). This same law stated that the history of African American, Polish, Lithuanian, German, Hungarian, Irish, Bohemian, Russian, Albanian, Italian, Czech, Slovak, French, Scot, Hispanic, and Asian American peoples, among others, should be included. In addition, Hernendez (2019) explained that there have been "other small changes to the language of the Illinois School Code.

Textbooks bought by the state government for Illinois public schools must now be completely non-discriminatory according to standards set in the Illinois Human Rights Act" (para. 2). Finally, in 2021, Illinois passed the Culturally Responsive Teaching and Learning Standards, which focus on closing the achievement gap through purposefully embedding cultural responsiveness in teacher education programs.

Although Illinois is just one example, it is important to know the mandates within your state to ensure equitable practices are embedded or to advocate for more equitable practices if they are not present.

12

Epilogue
Keep the Momentum Going

"Just keep moving. Just keep moving. . . ."

Whether you have full support from the whole team, including administrators, or partial support from the wider organization, revisiting the foundational work described throughout this book is important for continued growth and learning. The work is not easy. You will have pushback, sometimes even from yourself as a coach. There have been multiple times in this work we have had to stop and reflect on our own biases and check ourselves or "call each other into" a conversation to keep our own growth momentum going. Regardless of who the inevitable pushback is coming from, it is important to take a step back, digest the uncomfortable feelings, process them, and then keep moving forward. You will never have 100% of the team at the exact same spot in their learning journeys. The important part is that you do not leave anyone too far behind but help in the growth journey of individuals, regardless of the path they are taking up the mountainside.

At this point, as the book is coming to a close and your head is full and spinning of new, old, and sometimes life-changing information, we would like to take the time to answer some frequently asked questions (FAQs).

How does a coach discuss topics and show videos that may be triggering or retraumatizing to groups of people?

Some of the videos and discussions can be traumatizing or retraumatizing to individuals. It is extremely important to provide a brief overview and trigger warning, with the option of not watching with no penalty. A trigger warning is "a statement made prior to sharing potentially disturbing content. That content might include graphic references to topics such as sexual abuse, self-harm, violence, eating disorders, and so on, and can take the form of an image, video clip, audio clip, or piece of text" (University of Waterloo, n.d., para. 1).

How often should the whole group come back to evaluate the organization based on the Anti-Ism Scale?

The organization should be evaluated one time per year. This will affect the overall strategic plan for the equity-focused work. A further recommendation is to add the equity-focused work as an objective within the school improvement plan (SIP) or strategic plan for focused support and learning.

How often should the whole group come back together to discuss, learn, and continue to grow?

The group should come together throughout the year. The minimum should be once every 6 months, but we recommend meeting as a whole group more often.

What if there are members of the organization who refuse to communicate and engage in the work?

There is not one answer for this question. Decisions regarding what to do in this situation need to be made by the organization. However, it is important to note that just because someone is not vocal or may appear to be inactively participating, that does not mean they are not learning. Some people process best through silence and reflection before engaging with others.

Should the Diversity Workgroup change members?

Yes and no. If the group has good rapport and is making progress, it is recommended to keep the same group. However, it is important that the Diversity Workgroup is not a closed committee but can welcome in new members. If there is no financial support to add to the committee size, then it is recommended to offer a reconfiguration of the Diversity Workgroup every year or every other year.

How will new staff members gain information regarding the implementation of equity-focused, transformative curriculum and wider practices?

The key areas that are important to the wider work and classroom implementation should be added to the onboarding packet for new staff members. They should also be provided with information about the Diversity Workgroup and any other small groups that are meeting as an optional way to engage in the work. Small groups could include affinity groups or book clubs.

What if my administration does not support this? Can I still do some of this work?

YES! Absolutely yes. There are many things within your locus of control, including the Harvard Implicit Association Test (easily found on Google) or self-assessment using a tool similar to the one in Figure 12.1.

APPENDIX C ENVIRONMENTAL SCAN SCORING GUIDE

Purpose: The purpose of diversity, equity, inclusion, access, and belonging assessment of the organization is to provide insights and recommendations for creating a culturally responsive environment to reach the needs of all employees and visitors/members.

Representation: Determines the extent to which individuals are reflected in an environment (visual and auditory).

Physical, Events, Written, and Internet Assessed.

The evaluation key for the rubrics is:
- None = 0% (missing in 10 or more spaces)
- Limited = 25% (missing in 8–10 spaces)
- Some = 50% (missing in 5–7 spaces)
- Moderate = 75% (missing in 2–4 spaces)
- Embedded = 100% (missing in 0–1 space)

When observing, please take detailed notes and take pictures (not of families or children) for documentation purposes. These documentation notes and photos should be included when turning in the evaluation for analysis.

Specific areas to evaluate for physical environment: Centers

Physical environment					
	1	2	3	4	5
Gender diversity	None	Limited	Some	Moderate	Embedded
Racial/ethnic diversity	None	Limited	Some	Moderate	Embedded
Religions/nonreligious diversity	None	Limited	Some	Moderate	Embedded
Linguistic diversity	None	Limited	Some	Moderate	Embedded
Age diversity	None	Limited	Some	Moderate	Embedded
Family diversity	None	Limited	Some	Moderate	Embedded
Career diversity	None	Limited	Some	Moderate	Embedded
Ability/disability diversity	None	Limited	Some	Moderate	Embedded

The artifacts to consider for the physical environment scan, include, but are not limited to, posters, pictures, level of materials (e.g., Are the smocks for the water table accessible to all ages?), noise level or noise cancelation ability, and the overall layout of the materials. Specific to the store: everything already listed as well as socioeconomic diversity (cost of items).

Figure 12.1. Environmental scan scoring guide. (From Reinking, A. [2022]. Diversity and Equity Environmental Scan; reprinted by permission.) (*Note:* A blank version of this form is available in Appendix C and to download.)

What if you have tried "everything" and it didn't work?

The first thing to remember is that it takes time. This is a multiyear process, with this book outlining the first year or so. Second, just because it did not "work" does not mean you stop trying. As a reminder, the preschool class of 2020 was the first class where BIPOC+ students were the majority. Therefore, continuing to implement practices in early childhood classrooms that are historically centered around White, heteronormative, Christian ideals will not reach all students. So, who are you willing to exclude or discriminate against in your classroom? No one! Therefore, if you have tried this work and have failed, take the words of Brené Brown and learn from your failure. Fail forward, identify the missteps, and try again with new action steps.

MOVING FORWARD WITH ADMINISTRATOR SUPPORT

Administrator support is needed to guide the work of the whole program. However, before diving into this more robust work, it is imperative that every person on this journey embeds an asset-based mindset, which at times is hard. As a group of collaborative learners, it is also important to keep each other accountable in the asset-based mindset, along with being honest.

Once that is established, you can focus on diving deeper into the zones of comfort from an antiracist viewpoint, which will then lead to other antiism discussions; honestly investigating institutional -isms within your wider school and community system in order to advocate for change; and becoming a change agent in the systemic issues that arise in this work and the wider community.

Figure 12.2 should look familiar. We have seen the zone of comfort or growth in Chapter 4 focused on overall learning. However, Figure 12.2 guides all of us to honestly reflect on becoming antiracist, which will lead to addressing other -isms that arise in our work as educators and as citizens in the wider community. When we are aware of our zone and work toward growth, we are able to enhance our visibility as agents of change in our schools and wider community.

Finally, honestly investigating systemic issues that arise in the work and wider community is imperative to continue the movement up the mountain. Systemic means that systems within our communities have been built on discriminatory practices that perpetuate unequal treatment. As seen in Figure 12.3, there are many aspects that affect systemic -isms within our programs and wider communities. Investigate what each of the terms in the figure means, in relation to systemic issues, and document the next steps your program can take to become agents of change.

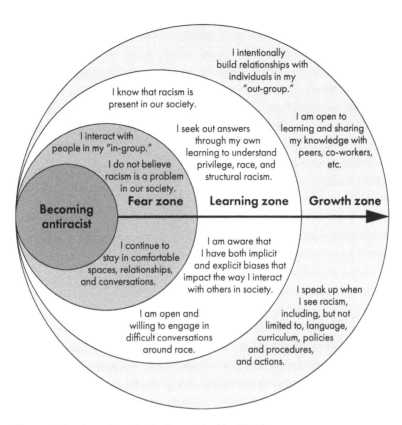

Figure 12.2. Becoming antiracist. (*Source:* Ibrahim, 2022.)

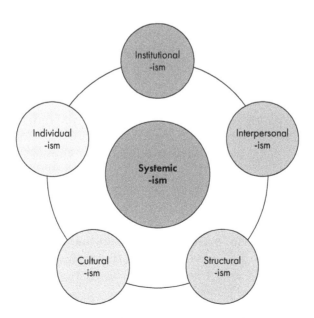

Figure 12.3. Systemic -isms. (*Source:* Figueroa's Framework, Figueroa, 1993.)

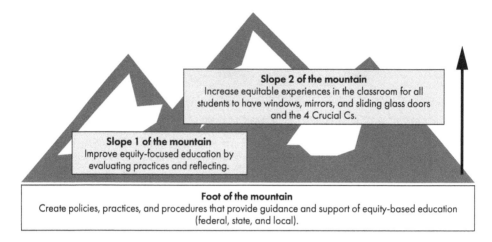

Figure 12.4. The DEIAB trajectory.

CLIMBING THE MOUNTAINSIDE

Climbing the mountain of equity-focused education is hard work, but making progress at each step, even if we must fail forward, is forward momentum in the direction of supporting all students. In Figure 12.4, the progress at each portion of the mountain is outlined. Before we can begin the work, or sometimes at the starting point of the work, policies and procedures need to be put into place to support the educators putting the work into creating equitable classroom environments.

After policies are developed, it is easier to move up the mountain to the first slope where educators and administrators can evaluate the current practices using the Anti-Ism Scale. Organizations and individuals can then progress to the second slope where classrooms are truly transformed, as described throughout this book, as a way to create equity for all students, families, and colleagues. Although the movement is up the mountain, it is important to remember that we sometimes may slide down. In other words, organizations and individuals slide between and among all three of the parts of the mountain but should always be striving for the summit.

Through reading this book and implementing the practices provided in these pages and the individualized work being completed at the ground level with educators, it is assumed you have felt the movement up, down, sideways, and maybe even backward on individual paths along the mountainside. Although we will never summit the mountain of DEIAB in our lifetime, we can each continue our transformational learning journey. So, just keeping moving.

References

Abdill, A. M. (2016). *There's a problem with this image and it's not what you think: The insidiousness of implicit bias*. LinkedIn. https://www.linkedin.com/pulse/problem-image-its-what-you-think-insidiousness-implicit-abdill/

Alberts, H., Houston, E., Poole, P., Schultz, J., Celestine, N., Sutton, J., Madeson, M., Page, O., Davis, D., Nortje, A., Vowell, C., Lonczak, H. S., Swainston, J., Neuhaus, M., Lancia, G., Schaffner, A. K., Gaines, J. J., & Bourne, J. (n.d.). *Positive Psychology Toolkit*. Positive Psychology.

Ali, S. (2020, July 31). I'm the only Black person in my office, here's what I wish my coworkers knew. *Reader's Digest*. https://www.rd.com/article/im-the-only-black-person-in-my-office/

Allen-Hughes, L. (2013). *The social benefits of the morning meeting: Creating a space for social and character education in the classroom* [Unpublished master's thesis]. Dominican University of California.

Aloneindarknes7. (n.d.) *Insufferably tolerant science nerd*. https://m.facebook.com/Insufferable Intolerance/photos/a.270237376470721/2428515037309600/

Annette. (2019, May 21). Fighting fears: Fear of not being liked. *Rise and Lead*. https://riseandlead.blog/2019/05/21/fear-of-not-being-liked/

Aronson, B., & Meyers, L. (2020). Critical race theory and the teacher education curriculum: Challenging understandings of racism, whiteness, and white supremacy. *Whiteness and Education*, 7(1), 1–26. https://doi.org/10.1080/23793406.2020.1812109

Arroyo, M. (2020, August 31). *Why "Hispanic/Latino" isn't a racial category on the U.S. Census*. IDEALS Institute. https://ideals.uark.edu/why-hispanic-latino-isnt-a-racial-category-on-the-u-s-census/

Audeliss. (n.d.). *Why people are uncomfortable talking about race at work*. https://www.audeliss.com/en/news/why-people-are-uncomfortable-talking-about-race-at-work/

Baldridge, J. [TEDx Talks]. (2018, April 11). *Difficult conversations made easy* [Video]. YouTube. https://www.youtube.com/watch?v=4TkbHLD5Mnw

Banks, J. A. (1999). *An introduction to multicultural education* (2nd ed.). Allyn and Bacon.

Belsha, K. (2021, September 27). *Students are struggling with behavior. Here's how schools are responding*. Chalkbeat. https://www.chalkbeat.org/2021/9/27/22691601/student-behavior-stress-trauma-return

Bettner, B. L., & Lew, A. (1990). *Raising kids who can*. Connections Press.

Bishop, R. S. (1990). Mirrors, windows, and sliding glass doors. *Perspectives: Choosing and Using Books for the Classroom*, 6(3), ix–xi.

Bradberry, T. (2018, November 13). *14 signs you are emotionally intelligent*. LinkedIn. https://www.linkedin.com/pulse/14-signs-youre-emotionally-intelligent-dr-travis-bradberry/

Brew, A. A. (2020, June 6). *Talk the talk: Strengthening your organization's diversity statement*. Nonprofit HR. https://www.nonprofithr.com/talk-the-talk-strengthening-your-organizations-diversity-statement/

Brown, C. T. (2021, November 3). *Arrested mobility: Exploring the impacts of over-policing Black mobility in the U.S.* Presentation on Cities@Tuffs. https://www.shareable.net/cities_tufts/arrested-mobility-exploring-the-impacts-of-over-policing-black-mobility-in-the-u-s/

Center for Creative Leadership. (2018). *Use active listening skills when coaching others.* https://www.ccl.org/articles/leading-effectively-articles/coaching-others-use-active-listening-skills/

Center of Great Teachers and Leaders. (2019). *Mentor selection criteria tally.* https://gtlcenter.org/sites/default/files/Module2-Workbook3-MentorSelectCriteriaTally.pdf

Clark, J. (2019, September 24). *How to balance equity, equality, and fairness.* Concordia University Irvine. https://www.cui.edu/academicprograms/education/perfecting-the-practice/blog/post/how-to-balance-equity-equality-and-fairness

Cole, N. (2019). *Understanding intersectionality and why it matters to sociologists.* ThoughtCo. https://www.thoughtco.com/intersectionality-definition-3026353#:~:text=However%2C%20intersectionality%20is%20not%20just%20useful%20for%20understanding

Coleman, A.L. (2019, March 29). *What's intersectionality? Let these scholars explain the theory and its history.* Time. https://time.com/5560575/intersectionality-theory/

Connell, R. W., & Messerschmidt, J. W. (2005). Hegemonic masculinity: Rethinking the concept. *Gender & Society, 19*(6), 829–859. https://doi.org/10.1177/0891243205278639

CROWN Coalition. (2019). *About—The Official CROWN Act.* https://www.thecrownact.com/about#:~:text=The%20CROWN%20Act%2C%20which%20stands%20for%20%E2%80%9CCreating%20a

Cuncic, A. (2021, September 21). *What is the difference between Hispanic and Latino?* Verywell Mind. https://www.verywellmind.com/what-is-the-difference-between-hispanic-vs-latino-5082005

Daskal, L. (2017). *The leadership gap: What gets between you and your greatness.* Portfolio Media.

Davis, A. M. (2021, February 23). *Diversity, equity, and inclusion have failed. How about belonging, dignity, and justice instead?* World Economic Forum. https://www.weforum.org/agenda/2021/02/diversity-equity-inclusion-have-failed-belonging-dignity-justice/

Derman-Sparks, L., & Edwards, J. O. (2010). *Anti-bias education for young children and ourselves* (Vol. 254). National Association for the Education of Young Children.

Derman-Sparks, L., Edwards, J. O., & Goins, C. M. (2020). *Anti-bias education: For young children and ourselves* (2nd ed.). National Association for the Education of Young Children.

Derman-Sparks, L., LeeKeenan, D., & Nimmo, J. (2015). *Leading anti-bias early childhood programs: A guide for change (early childhood education).* Teachers College Press.

Diversity, Equity, and Inclusion—Glossary of Equity-Related Terms, Version 3. (2022). https://ofm.wa.gov/sites/default/files/public/shr/Diversity/SubCommit/DEIGlossaryofEquityRelatedTerms.pdf

Doeing, D. (2019, May 9). *Craft the perfect diversity statement for your organization.* Learn.g2.com. https://learn.g2.com/diversity-statement#:~:text=A%20diversity%20statement%20for%20your%20organization%20is%20a

Dunn, J. L. (2021, February 3). *Learning for justice: Teaching Tolerance changes its name to reflect evolving work in the struggle for radical change in education and community.* Southern Poverty Law Center. https://www.splcenter.org/news/2021/02/03/learning-justice-teaching-tolerance-changes-its-name-reflect-evolving-work-struggle-radical

Ellemers, N., & Rink, F. (2016). Diversity in work groups. *Current Opinion in Psychology, 11,* 49–53.

EnglishXP. (2021). *Objective vs subjective language.* English XP. https://englishxp.co.uk/grammar/objective-vs-subjective-language/

Epoch Education. (2021). *Recognizing microaggressions activity.* https://epocheducation.com/wp-content/uploads/2021/03/microaggressions_tool_final-2021.pdf

Ferber, M. A., & Nelson, J. A. (Eds.). (2009). *Beyond economic man: Feminist theory and economics.* University of Chicago Press.

Figueroa, P. (1993). *Equality, multiculturalism, antiracism and physical education in the national curriculum.* Routledge.

Ford, C. L., & Airhihenbuwa, C. O. (2009). Critical race theory, race equity, and public health: Toward antiracism praxis. *American Journal of Public Health, 100*(S1), S30–S35. https://doi.org/10.2105/ajph.2009.171058

Galiana, D. (2019, October 28). *The 5W1H method: Project management defined and applied.* Wimi Teamwork. https://www.wimi-teamwork.com/blog/the-5w1h-method-project-management-defined-and-applied/

Gannon, M. (2016). Race is a social construct, scientists argue. *Scientific American.* https://www.scientificamerican.com/article/race-is-a-social-construct-scientists-argue/

Gillies J. (2014). Critical disability theory. In A. C. Michalos (Ed.), *Encyclopedia of quality of life and well-being research*. Springer. https://link.springer.com/referenceworkentry/10.1007/978-94-007-0753-5_619

Gjelten, E. A. (2019, February 5). *What are zero tolerance policies in schools?* Lawyers.com. https://www.lawyers.com/legal-info/research/education-law/whats-a-zero-tolerance-policy.html

Glossary for Educational Reform. (2015). *Hidden curriculum*. https://www.edglossary.org/hidden-curriculum/

Gordon Training International. (n.d.). *The roadblocks to communication*. Gordonmodel.com. http://www.gordonmodel.com/home-roadblocks.php

Great Schools Partnership. (2013a, May 15). *Multicultural education definition*. The Glossary of Education Reform. https://www.edglossary.org/multicultural-education/

Great Schools Partnership. (2013b, August 29). *At-risk definition*. The Glossary of Education Reform. https://www.edglossary.org/at-risk/

Green, E., Ropars, E., & Reinking, A. (Hosts). (2021). Adult anti-bias education [Audio podcast episode]. In *STAR NET regions I&III podcast*. Apple. https://podcasts.apple.com/us/podcast/star-net-regions-i-iii-podcast/id1531496692

Hall, J. M. (2018). Philosophy of dance and disability. *Philosophy Compass, 13*(12), e12551. https://doi.org/10.1111/phc3.12551

Hall, K. (2014, March 24). Create a sense of belonging. *Psychology Today*. https://www.psychologytoday.com/us/blog/pieces-mind/201403/create-sense-belonging

Hammond, W. (2010). *Principles of strength-based practice*. Resiliency Initiatives. https://greaterfallsconnections.org/wp-content/uploads/2014/07/Principles-of-Strength-2.pdf

Harro, B. (2000). The Cycle of Socialization. *Readings for Diversity and Social Justice, 2*, 45–51.

Heaslip, E. (2020, August 18). *How to write a diversity and inclusion statement*. U.S. Chamber of Commerce. https://www.uschamber.com/co/start/strategy/writing-diversity-and-inclusion-statement

Heinrich, R., Molenda, M., Russell, J. D., & Smaldino, S. E. (1996). *Instructional media and technologies for learning*. Merrill.

Hernendez, W. (2019, October 23). *Illinois public schools to include LGBTQ history*. NextLevel Law, P.C. https://www.nextlevel.law/blog/2019/10/illinois-public-schools-to-include-lgbtq-history/

Hopper, E. (2019). *What is a microaggression? Everyday insults with harmful effects*. ThoughtCo. https://www.thoughtco.com/microaggression-definition-examples-4171853

Hunt, D. (2020, June 25). *Some do's and don'ts for White people who want to discuss racism at work*. ZORA. https://zora.medium.com/5-dos-and-dont-s-for-white-leaders-and-colleagues-who-want-to-discuss-racism-at-work-ff8f83799665

Ibrahim, A. M. (2022). A surgeon's journey through research and design. *SurgeryRedesign*. www.surgeryredesign.com

Jackson, A. (2019, August 11). *LGBTQ history curriculum will now be taught in Illinois schools*. CNN. https://www.cnn.com/2019/08/11/us/illinois-lgbtq-history-curriculum-trnd/index.html

Jewell, T. (2020). *This book is anti-racist: 20 lessons on how to wake up, take action, and do the work*. Quarto Publishing Group.

Kearsley, G. (2010). *Andragogy (M. Knowles)*. The Theory Into Practice Database. 17 tips to motivate adult learners—eLearning Industry. https://elearningindustry.com/17-tips-to-motivate-adult-learners

Kelly, R. (2018, July 26). *10 examples of awesome diversity statements*. Ongig Blog. https://blog.ongig.com/diversity-and-inclusion/10-examples-of-the-best-diversity-statements/

Klein, C. (2013, March 8). *Learn about communication blocks so parents can improve connection*. Bridges 2 Understanding. https://bridges2understanding.com/learn-about-communication-blocks-so-parents-can-improve-connection/

Knowles, E. D., Lowery, B. S., Chow, R. M., & Unzueta, M. M. (2014). Deny, distance, or dismantle? How White Americans manage a privileged identity. *Perspectives on Psychological Science, 9*(6), 594–609. https://doi.org/10.1177/1745691614554658

Krogstad, J. M. (2019, July 31). *A view of the nation's future through kindergarten demographics*. Pew Research Center. https://www.pewresearch.org/facttank/2019/07/31/kindergarten-demographics-in-us

Kuttner, P. (2015). *The problem with the equity vs. equality graphic you're using*. Cultural Organizing. https://www.socialventurepartners.org/wp-content/uploads/2018/01/Problem-with-Equity-vs-Equality-Graphic.pdf

Maeda, J. (2019). *Design in Tech Report 2019*. Design in Tech.

Malik, S. (2015, April 23). *How to overcome the major challenges in cross cultural communication*. Audeliss. https://www.linkedin.com/pulse/how-overcome-major-challenges-cross-cultural-iim-shillong-pgpex/

McIntosh, P. (2000). Interactive phases of personal and curricular re-vision with regard to race. In G. Shin & P. Gorski (Eds.), *Multicultural resource series: Professional development for educators*. National Education Association.

McManis, L. D. (2021). *Inclusive education: What it means, proven strategies, and a case study*. Resilient Educator. https://resilienteducator.com/classroom-resources/inclusive-education/

Moll, L., Amanti, C., Neff, D., & Gonzalez, N. (1992). Funds of knowledge for teaching: using a qualitative approach to connect home and classrooms. *Qualitative Issues in Educational Research, 31*, 132–141.

Montoya, E. (2021, March 9). *The effects of microaggressions on one's health*. Morning Sign Out. https://sites.uci.edu/morningsignout/2021/03/09/the-effects-of-microaggressions-on-ones-health

Morgan, K. P. (1996). Describing the emperor's new clothes: Three myths of education (in)equality. In A. Diller (Ed.), *The gender question in education, theory, pedagogy and politics*. Westview. https://elearningindustry.com/17-tips-to-motivate-adult-learners

NAACP Legal Defense and Educational Fund. (2019). *Doctors Kenneth and Mamie Clark and "The Doll Test."* https://www.naacpldf.org/brown-vs-board/significance-doll-test/

Nieto, S. (2008). Affirmation, solidarity and critique: Moving beyond tolerance in education. In E. Lee, D. Menkart, & M. Okazawa-Rey (Eds.), *Beyond heroes and holidays* (pp. 18–29). Teaching for Change.

Pappas, C. (2013, May 9). *The adult learning theory—andragogy—of Malcolm Knowles*. eLearning Industry. http://elearningindustry.com/the-adult-learning-theory-andragogy-of-malcolm-knowles

Picture Alternatives. (2019, November 12). *Our hidden biases* [Video]. https://www.youtube.com/watch?v=ZWgVs4qj1ho

Popkin, M. (2003). *Active parenting now: For parents of children ages 5 to 12. The basics*. Active Parenting.

Queensborough Community College. (2020). *Definition for diversity*. https://academyofcreativecoaching.com/definition-for-diversity

Regional Educational Laboratory Southwest. (2019). *Strategies for recruiting a diverse teacher workforce*. https://ies.ed.gov/ncee/edlabs/regions/southwest/pdf/infographics/RELSW-Teacher-Diversity-508.pdf

Reinking, A. (2019). *Difficult conversations: A toolkit for educators in handling real-life situations*. Rowman & Littlefield.

Reinking (2020). (February 26, 2021). https://www.instagram.com/p/CLxnPhUBiFg/

Responsive Classroom. (2016, June 7). *What is morning meeting?* https://www.responsiveclassroom.org/what-is-morning-meeting/

Rise. (2021, August 10). *Team building icebreakers for returning to the office*. https://risepeople.com/blog/team-building-icebreakers/

Robinson, L., Segal, J., & Smith, M. (2019, March 21). *Effective communication*. HelpGuide. https://www.helpguide.org/articles/relationships-communication/effective-communication.htm

Russell, J. (2009). *Surviving difficult conversations*. Russell Consulting.

Sarkis, S. A. (2017). 11 warning signs of gaslighting. *Psychology Today*. https://www.psychologytoday.com/us/blog/here-there-and-everywhere/201701/11-warning-signs-gaslighting

Scarbrough, E. (2021, October 28). Professor discusses why many popular Halloween costumes are examples of cultural misappropriation. *FIU News*. https://news.fiu.edu/2021/halloween-costumes-and-cultural-appropriation

Solorzano, D. G. (1997). Images and words that wound: Critical race theory, racial stereotyping, and teacher education. *Teacher Education Quarterly, 24*(3), 5–19. http://www.jstor.org/stable/23478088

Souto-Manning, M. *Multicultural teaching in the early childhood classroom: Approaches, strategies, and tools, preschool–2nd grade*. Teacher's College Press.

Special Education Resource. (2020, January 14). *What are accommodations and modifications in special education?* https://specialedresource.com/accommodations-and-modifications-in-special-education

Swartz, T. H., Palermo, A. G. S., Masur, S. K., & Aberg, J. A. (2019). The science and value of diversity: Closing the gaps in our understanding of inclusion and diversity. *The Journal of Infectious Diseases, 220*(2), S33–S41.

Tajfel, H., & Turner, J. C. (1979). An integrative theory of intergroup conflict. In W. G. Austin & S. Worchel (Eds.), *The social psychology of intergroup relations* (pp. 33–37). Brooks/Cole.

Teaching for Change. (2022). *Anti-bias education.* https://www.teachingforchange.org/educator-resources/anti-bias-education

TeachThought Staff. (2018, December 17). *100+ Bloom's Taxonomy verbs for critical thinking.* TeachThought. https://www.teachthought.com/critical-thinking/blooms-taxonomy-verbs/

The Trevor Project. (n.d). *"Coming Out" stars activity.* https://www.thetrevorproject.org/wp-content/uploads/2017/08/75ea657f061737b608_6pm6ivozp.pdf

Thompson, A. K. (2017, November 9). *The hidden curriculum and school ethos.* ReviseSociology. https://revisesociology.com/2017/11/09/the-hidden-curriculum-and-school-ethos

Ting-Toomey, S. (1999). *Communicating across cultures.* Guilford Press.

University of Michigan (n.d.). Social Identity Wheel. *Peace, Love, and Dance.* https://digitalresearch.bsu.edu/peacelovedancebsu/items/show/10

University of Nebraska Omaha. (n.d.). *Queer and trans spectrum definitions.* https://www.unomaha.edu/student-life/inclusion/gender-and-sexuality-resource-center/lgbtqia-resources/queer-trans-spectrum-definitions.php

University of Waterloo. (n.d.). *Trigger warnings.* Centre for Teaching Excellence. https://uwaterloo.ca/centre-for-teaching-excellence/trigger

Upchurch, A. (2021, March). *The Cycle of Socialization and liberation.* The Justice Beat Talk Show. https://www.thejusticebeat.com/post/the-cycle-of-socialization-liberation

U.S. Department of Commerce and Vice President Al Gore's National Partnership for Reinventing Government Benchmarking study. (2001). Best Practices in Achieving Workforce Diversity. Retrieved from https://govinfo.library.unt.edu/npr/library/workforce-diversity.pdf

WGBH Educational Foundation. (2014). *Module: Honoring diversity.* Resources for Early Learning. http://resourcesforearlylearning.org/educators/module/20/12/56/

Willen, E., & Allan, C. (2021, February 11). *Understanding implicit bias, and why it affects kids.* Children's Mercy. https://www.childrensmercy.org/parent-ish/2021/02/implicit-bias/

Willingham, A. (2019, March 21). *Researchers studied nearly 100 million traffic stops and found Black motorists are more likely to be pulled over.* CNN. https://www.cnn.com/2019/03/21/us/police-stops-race-stanford-study-trnd/index.html

Worthy, L., Lavigne, T., & Romero, F. (2020). *Culture and Psychology.* Maricopa Open Digital Press.

Zyzdryn, A. (2020, December 8). *Not all Mexicans speak Spanish!* Legal Interpreters LLC. http://legal-interpreters.com/blog/not-all-mexicans-speak-spanish/2020/12/08

APPENDIX A   PROFESSIONAL AND ORGANIZATION CRITERIA CHECKLIST

Attitude and character					
Criteria	Y	N	N/A	Explanation	Notes
Does the professional or organization exhibit a strong commitment to the teaching profession?					
Does the professional or organization demonstrate friendly and positive behavior to others?					
Is this professional or organization resilient and flexible?					
Is the professional or organization willing to share knowledge and information with coworkers?					
Does the professional or organization model accountability and ownership?					
Does the professional or organization model continuous learning?					
Does the professional or organization recognize their own limitations?					
Does the professional or organization keep an optimistic attitude about people?					

(*Source:* Center of Great Teachers and Leaders, 2019.)

APPENDIX A (continued)

Professional competence and experience					
Criteria	Y	N	N/A	Explanation	Notes
Is the professional or organization knowledgeable on the topics of diversity, equity, inclusion, access, and belonging (DEIAB)?					
Does the professional or organization critically reflect on their practices and make adjustments to fit the needs of their students?					
Does the professional or organization collaborate well with colleagues, families, and administrators?					
Does the professional or organization support learning for diverse learners?					
Does the professional or organization have a history of exemplary evaluations?					
Is the professional or organization able to scaffold support over time?					

(Source: Center of Great Teachers and Leaders, 2019.)

APPENDIX A *(continued)*

Communication skills					
Criteria	Y	N	N/A	Explanation	Notes
Does the professional or organization have clear communication strategies (written and verbal)?					
Does the professional or organization provide positive and constructive feedback?					
Does the professional or organization use common courtesies (e.g., please, thank you)?					
Does the professional or organization listen more than talk?					

(Source: Center of Great Teachers and Leaders, 2019.)

APPENDIX A (continued)

Interpersonal skills					
Criteria	Y	N	N/A	Explanation	Notes
Does the professional or organization work well with people who do not share their identity or cultural background?					
Does the professional or organization apologize for mistakes or for treating others without respect?					
Does the professional or organization confront the issue, not the person?					
Does the professional or organization remain curious rather than defensive?					
Does the professional or organization help others view mistakes as learning opportunities?					

(Source: Center of Great Teachers and Leaders, 2019.)

APPENDIX B   PROFESSIONAL LEARNING GOALS DOCUMENTATION

Teacher name: _____

Supervisor/teacher coach: _____

Date: _____

Professional goal setting

Goals	Next steps	Resources/support needed
Goal 1		
Goal 2		
Goal 3		

Goals must be actionable and measurable.

APPENDIX C ENVIRONMENTAL SCAN SCORING GUIDE

Purpose: The purpose of diversity, equity, inclusion, access, and belonging assessment of the organization is to provide insights and recommendations for creating a culturally responsive environment to reach the needs of all employees and visitors/members.

Representation: Determines the extent to which individuals are reflected in an environment (visual and auditory).

Physical, Events, Written, and Internet Assessed.

The evaluation key for the rubrics is:
- None = 0% (missing in 10 or more spaces)
- Limited = 25% (missing in 8–10 spaces)
- Some = 50% (missing in 5–7 spaces)
- Moderate = 75% (missing in 2–4 spaces)
- Embedded = 100% (missing in 0–1 space)

When observing, please take detailed notes and take pictures (not of families or children) for documentation purposes. These documentation notes and photos should be included when turning in the evaluation for analysis.

Specific areas to evaluate for physical environment: Centers

Physical environment	1	2	3	4	5
Gender diversity	None	Limited	Some	Moderate	Embedded
Racial/ethnic diversity	None	Limited	Some	Moderate	Embedded
Religions/nonreligious diversity	None	Limited	Some	Moderate	Embedded
Linguistic diversity	None	Limited	Some	Moderate	Embedded
Age diversity	None	Limited	Some	Moderate	Embedded
Family diversity	None	Limited	Some	Moderate	Embedded
Career diversity	None	Limited	Some	Moderate	Embedded
Ability/disability diversity	None	Limited	Some	Moderate	Embedded

The artifacts to consider for the physical environment scan include, but are not limited to, posters, pictures, level of materials (e.g., Are the smocks for the water table accessible to all ages?), noise level or noise cancelation ability, and the overall layout of the materials. Specific to the store: everything already listed as well as socioeconomic diversity (cost of items).

From Reinking, A. (2022). Diversity and Equity Environmental Scan; reprinted by permission.

Index

Page numbers followed by *t* and *f* indicate tables and figures, respectively.

ABCD Method, 78, 90
Abdill, Aasha M., 6
ABE, *see* Antibias education
Acceptance level of support for multicultural education, 125
Access, 13
Accommodations, 13
Accountability, in Diversity Workgroups, 107–109
Action plans
 in coaching, 50
 in Diversity Workgroups, 107, 108*f*, 109*f*, 112
Action verbs, 78, 80*f*
Active listening, 37, 37*f*, 38*t*
Additive Approach, 124, 128
Administrators
 activities without support of, 141
 letters about program integration to, 133, 135*f*
 moving forward with support of, 142
Adult learning theory, 45–46, 91
Affinity groups, 119–121
Age, in Social Identity Wheel, 25
Agendas
 for coaching meetings, 53–54, 53*f*
 for first training workshops, 77–86, 94, 95*f*
American history
 exclusion in, 3, 4
 state laws on teaching of, 137
Andragogy, *see* Adult learning theory
Antibias education (ABE)
 continuum of change in, 55
 definition of, xvii–xviii, 6
 diversity in, 6

in diversity statements, 103, 105
goals of, xviii, 29, 121
Antibullying policies, 131
Anti-Ism Action Plan, 107, 108*f*
Anti-Ism Scale, 60–73, 61*f*
 annual revisiting of, 140
 coaching to, 73–74
 description of ratings on, 63–73
 in Diversity Workgroups, 105–106
 at first training workshops, 94, 95*f*
 goal setting based on, 106–107
 origins of, 60
 purpose of, 60–63
Anti-Racism Scale, 60
Antiracists, path to becoming, 142, 143*f*
Apple tree graphic, 8–9, 8*f*
Asset-based mindset, 121, 136, 142
At risk, use of term, 28

"Bad students," 131
Baldridge, Joy, 51
Band-Aid activity, 9–10
Banks, J. A., 60, 124
Beginner teachers, 55, 56, 58
Beginner's mindset, 91
Behavior constraints, 34
Bell, Derrick, xvi
Bell, W. Kamau, 35
Belonging
 definition of, 13–16
 4 Crucial Cs of, 14–16, 15*f*
 Morning Meetings and, 87–90
Belonging, justice, and dignity (BJD), 16

Bettner, Betty Lou, 14–15
Biases, explicit, 82
 see also Implicit biases
BIPOC+
 affinity groups for, 120–121
 burden of diversity discussions on, 101
 creating inclusive environments for, 101
 as majority in class of 2020, 142
 use of term, 22
Bishop, R. S., 17–18
BJD, *see* Belonging, justice, and dignity
Black, Indigenous, and People of Color, *see* BIPOC+
Black people
 affinity groups for, 120–121
 burden of diversity discussions on, 101
 disciplinary policies and, 131
 impacts of segregation on, 118
 language of, 24–25
 use of term, 22
 see also BIPOC+
Bloom's taxonomy, 78, 80*f*
Boards of directors, 131
Book study groups, 121
Books
 banned, 131, 137
 hidden curricula in, 83–84, 84*f*–85*f*
 state laws and mandates on, 137–138
Bradberry, Travis, 30
Bravery, in community agreements, 90
Brown, Brené, 45, 87, 142
Brown, Charles T., 72
Brown people
 affinity groups for, 120–121

156

Index

burden of diversity
  discussions on, 101
disciplinary policies and, 131
use of term, 22
see also BIPOC+
Bullying policies, 131

Cs, 4 Crucial, 14–16, 15*f*
Calling in vs. calling out,
  19–20, 38, 40–41
Calm down corners, 14
Capable, in belonging, 14–15,
  15*f*
Caucasian, use of term, 21–22,
  92
Census, U.S., 22
Center on Great Teachers and
  Leaders, 46
Chocolate Me (Diggs), 39–40
Circle of Trust activity, 58
Cisgender, 23
Clark, J., 6
Clark, Kenneth, 118
Clark, Mamie, 118
Coaching, 45–58
  adult learning theory in,
    45–46
  to Anti-Ism Scale, 73–74
  barriers to, 51
  checklists for self-reflection
    in, 46, 47*f*–48*f*, 50, 50*f*,
    151*f*–154*f*
  feedback in, 49–50, 49*t*
  goals and timing of, 49, 49*t*
  meeting agendas in, 53–54,
    53*f*
  setting professional
    development goals in,
    52–58
  vs. supervising, 52, 53
Cognitive constraints, 34
Comfort
  lack of, as part of process,
    38–39
  zones of, 56–57, 57*f*, 142
Communication, 29–41
  active listening in, 37, 37*f*, 38*t*
  barriers and blocks to, 32–36
  emotional intelligence in,
    30–31
  kind vs. nice, 31–32, 32*t*
  through letters to families
    and administrators, 133,
    134*f*, 135*f*
  making progress through,
    38–41
  types of, 29–30
  see also Language
Communications, external, 132
Community agreements, 90–91
Community mapping, 135–137,
  136*f*
Confidentiality, in community
  agreements, 90

Connection, in belonging,
  14–16, 15*f*
Constructive feedback, 49, 49*t*
Contributions Approach, 124
Conversations, difficult, 31–33
  see also Communication
Coronavirus (COVID-19)
  pandemic, 34, 131
Counting, in belonging, 14–15,
  15*f*
Courage, in belonging, 14–16,
  15*f*
COVID-19 pandemic, 34, 131
Crenshaw, Kimberlee, 5
Critical disability theory, xvii
Critical race theory (CRT)
  backlash against, 126, 131
  definition and purpose of,
    xvi, 131
  state laws and mandates
    on, 137
Critical theories, xv–xvii, 20
CROWN Act, 130–131
CRT, *see* Critical race theory
Csikszentmihalyi, Mihaly, 29
Cultural appropriation, 81
Cultural diversity, as
  communication barrier,
    33–34
Cultural snacks, 113
Culturally Responsive
  Teaching and Learning
  Standards, 138
Cultures, high-context vs. low-
  context, 34
Cuncic, A., 22
Curriculum of the Mainstream
  Approach, 124
Cycle of Socialization, 115,
  116–118, 116*f*

DEIAB, *see* Diversity, Equity,
  Inclusion, Access, and
  Belonging
Derman-Sparks, L., xvii–xviii,
  6, 126
Difficult conversations, 31–33
Diggs, Taye, 39–40
Disability(ies)
  critical disability theory on,
    xvii
  definitions of, 25
  disciplinary policies and, 131
  purposeful language
    around, 25
  in Social Identity Wheel, 25
Disciplinary policies, 131
Discomfort, as part of process,
  38–39
Discrimination
  in school policies, 130–131
  social inequality and, 7
Distracting, communication
  block of, 35

Diversity
  definitions of, 5–6, 80*t*
  of social identities, xiii, 5
  of staff, ways of increasing,
    100–101, 131
  statements on, 103–105,
    104*f*
  types of, xiii
  see also specific types
Diversity, Equity, Inclusion,
  Access, and Belonging
  (DEIAB)
  definitions of, 5–16
  mountainside analogy for,
    xv, xv*f*, 3–4, 144, 144*f*
  theories associated with,
    xv–xvii
Diversity statements, 103–105,
  104*f*
Diversity Workgroups, 97–109
  action plans of, 107, 108*f*,
    109*f*, 112
  Anti-Ism Scale ratings in,
    105–106
  barriers to creating, 100–102
  benefits of, 98–99
  changes to membership of,
    140
  diversity statements of,
    103–105, 104*f*
  FAQs on, 140–141
  goal setting by, 106–109, 108*f*,
    109*f*
  meeting schedules for,
    102–103, 140
  positive group dynamics in,
    99–100
  in program integration,
    111–114
  purpose of, 97, 103
  requirements for, 97–98
  roles in, 103
Doeing, D., 103
Doll Test Study, 115, 118
Draw a Picture activity, 94
Drucker, Peter, 123
Dunn, Jalaya Lies, 67

Edwards, J. O., xviii
Emotional constraints, 34
Emotional intelligence, 30–31
Emotional responses, negative,
  36
Empathy, teaching
  activities for, 115
  challenges of, 4
  in multicultural education,
    126
English language, 24
Environmental scan scoring
  guide, 141*f*, 156*f*
Equality
  definition of, 8*f*
  vs. equity, 6–10, 7*f*, 8*f*

Equity
  definitions of, 6–10, 8f, 72
  vs. equality, 6–10, 7f, 8f
  Myths of, 17–18
Ethnicity
  definition of, 22
  vs. race, 22
  in Social Identity Wheel, 22
Exclusion, history of, 3, 4
Exclusive rating on Anti-Ism Scale, 63–66
Explicit biases, 82

"Failing forward," 16, 30, 45, 142
Fairness, teaching, 4, 126
Families
  activities at home for, 128–130
  letters about program integration to, 133, 134f
Family Flag activity, 11, 128–130, 129f
FAQs, 114, 114f, 139–142
Feedback, in coaching, 49–50, 49t
Feminist theory, xvi–xvii
Ferber, M. A., xvii
First language, in Social Identity Wheel, 24
5W1H questions, 78, 79f
Food, 113
Forbes, Malcolm, 97
4 Crucial Cs, 14–16, 15f
Frequently asked questions (FAQs), 114, 114f, 139–142
Funds of knowledge, 85–86

Games, in Morning Meetings, 89
Gannon, M., 21
Gary (Rudge), 39–40
Gaslighting, 36
Gender
  definition of, 23, 24f
  in Social Identity Wheel, 23
  of teachers, 62
Gender Unicorn, 23, 24f
Generational stereotypes, 25
Gillies, J., xvii
Goal setting
  based on Anti-Ism Scale, 106–107
  professional development, 52–58, 54f, 155f
  S.M.A.R.T., 54–55, 57, 107
Golden Rule, 14, 39
Great Schools Partnership, 28, 123
Green, Evelyn, 4
Greetings, in Morning Meetings, 88
Group dynamics, positive, 99–100

Group learning, *see* Workshops
Grow-Your-Own (GYO) programs, 131

Hair discrimination, 130–131
Halloween, 81
Handedness, 120
Harvard Implicit Association Test, 82, 141
Heaslip, E., 104
Hegemonic institutional prejudices, 64–69
Heinrich, R., 78
Hernandez, W., 137
Heroes and Holidays Approach, 124
Hidden Bias video, 115, 118–119
Hidden curriculum
  in Anti-Ism Scale, 65
  in books, 83–84, 84f–85f
  definition of, 11, 83
  as learning topic for workshops, 83–84
Hierarchy
  of Needs, 13, 14f
  organizational, 34
High-context cultures, 34
Hispanic, use of term, 22
Historically marginalized and oppressed identities, 60–62, 62t
Historically privileged identities, 60–62, 62t
History
  exclusion in, 3, 4
  state laws on teaching of, 137
Holidays
  cultural appropriation in, 81
  FAQs on, 114
  in multicultural curriculum, 124
  in program integration, 112
  religious, 65, 120, 124
Home activities, 128–130
Honesty, in community agreements, 90
Human capital, 85–86

"I," speaking from the, 91
Icebreakers, 87–90
Identities (social)
  critical theories on, xv–xvi, 20
  definition of, 5
  diversity of, xiii, 5
  intersectionality of, 5, 26–27, 26f
  purposeful language around, 20–25
  types of, 20
  see also specific types
Identity communication blocks, 36
Identity Wheel, *see* Social Identity Wheel

Identity/Affirming Change rating on Anti-Ism Scale, 70–72
Illinois, 137–138
Impact, vs. intent, 38–40
Implicit biases
  definition of, 81–82
  Harvard Implicit Association Test of, 82, 141
  in hidden curricula, 83
  as learning topic for workshops, 81–83
  in microaggressions, 82
  "Our Hidden Biases" video on, 115, 118–119
Inclusion
  definition of, 10–12
  state laws and mandates on, 137–138
  tips for creating environments of, 101
Inequality
  definition of, 8f
  social vs. structural, 7
In-groups
  in Circle of Trust activity, 58
  critical theories on, xvi, 20
Integration Stage, 124
  see also Program integration
Intelligence, emotional, 30–31
Intent
  assuming good, 91
  vs. impact, 38–40
Interrogating, communication block of, 35
Intersectionality, 5, 26–27, 26f
-Isms, 4, 142, 143f
  see also Anti-Ism Scale

Jewell, Tiffany, 21
Journaling, 94
Judging, communication block of, 36
Justice
  definition of, 8f
  restorative, 131

Kindness, vs. niceness, 31–32, 32t
Know-it-all, 36
Knowledge, funds of, 85–86
Knowles, E. D., 71
Knowles, Malcolm Shepherd, 45–46
Krishnamurti, Jiddu, 45
Kuttner, Paul, 6

Labeling, of "bad students," 131
Language
  as communication barrier, 33
  first, in Social Identity Wheel, 24

of leadership, 19
loaded words in, 85f
power of, 19
see also Communication
Language, purposeful, 19–28
definition of, 19–20
around identity, 20–25
intersectionality in, 26–27
subjective vs. objective, 27–28
Latino, use of term, 22
Laws, state, 137–138
Leadership
diversity of, 131
language of, 19
support for Diversity Workgroups in, 98
Learner teachers, 55, 56
Learning for Justice, 67
Lew, Amy, 14
LGBTQIA+ history, 137
LGBTQIA+ teachers, 67
Listening, active, 37, 37f, 38t
Loaded words, 85f
Low-context cultures, 34

Majority-minority threshold, 5
Male teachers, 62
Malik, S., 34
Mandates, state, 137–138
Mapping, community, 135–137, 136f
Marginalized and oppressed identities, historically, 60–62, 62t
Marketing, external, 132
Masculinity, hegemonic, 64
Maslow's Hierarchy of Needs, 13, 14f
McIntosh, P., 60, 124
McManis, L. D., 10
Meetings
coaching, 53–54, 53f
of Diversity Workgroups, 102–103, 140
morning, 87–90
Men, as teachers, 62
Mentimeter, 92–93, 93f
Mentor teachers, 55, 56
Messages, in Morning Meetings, 90
Microaggressions
in Anti-Ism Scale, 66
definition of, 66, 82
effects of, 83
as learning topic for workshops, 82–83
visual, 132
Mindset, asset-based, 121, 136, 142
Mirrors, metaphorical, 11, 12
Monocultural level of support for multicultural education, 125
Moore-Southall, Trina, 119

Moralizing, communication block of, 35
Morning Meetings, 87–90
Mountainside analogy, xv, xvf, 3–4, 144, 144f
Multicultural, Social Action, and Awareness Stage, 124–125
Multicultural education, 123–132
content of, 126–127
definition of, 123
delivery of, 126–127
Family Flag activity in, 128–130, 129f
levels of support for, 125
materials in, 127–128
school policies in, 130–131
staff diversity in, 131
stages of implementation of, 123–125
state laws and mandates on, 137–138

NAACP Legal Defense and Education Fund, 118
National origin, in Social Identity Wheel, 23
Needs, Maslow's Hierarchy of, 13, 14f
Negative emotional responses, 36
Nelson, J. A., xvii
Niceness, vs. kindness, 31–32, 32t
Nieto, S., 125
"No One Here Looks Like Me" (Thigpen), 102
Nonclosure, being okay with, 38, 41, 91
Normativity, 10

Objective language, 27–28
Observation, in coaching and supervising, 52–55
Onboarding packets, 141
One Word activity, 92
Opposition
to critical race theory, 126, 131
to program integration, 113–114, 133, 139
"Our Hidden Biases" video, 115, 118–119
Out-groups
in Circle of Trust activity, 58
critical theories on, xvi, 20

Passive/Tolerant rating on Anti-Ism Scale, 66–68
Peer journals, 94
Person of color (POC), use of term, 22
see also BIPOC+
Personal journals, 94

Perspectives, various, in Diversity Workgroups, 98–99
Physical barriers to communication, 34
Planning
how to start, 59–60
for program integration, 111–113, 112f
see also Action plans
Platinum Rule, 14, 39
POC, *see* Person of color
Policies, school, 130–131
Positive feedback, 49, 49t
Positive group dynamics, 99–100
Privileged identities, historically, 60–62, 62t
Professional and organization criteria checklist, 46, 47f–48f, 151f–154f
Professional development, setting goals for, 52–58, 54f, 155f
Professional learning goals documentation, 54, 54f, 155f
Program Apples case study, xiv, xix
Program integration, 111–121
activities supporting, 115–119
affinity groups in, 119–121
book studies in, 121
community mapping in, 135–137, 136f
FAQs for educators in, 114, 114f
planning for, 111–113, 112f
pushback against, 113–114, 133, 139
stalled, communicating about, 133, 134f, 135f
Purposeful language, *see* Language, purposeful

Queensborough Community College, 6
Queer theory, xvi–xvii
Questions
in conclusion activities, 94
5W1H, 78, 79f
frequently asked, 114, 114f, 139–142

Race
affinity groups based on, 119–121
definition of, 21
vs. ethnicity, 22
in hair discrimination, 130–131
purposeful language around, 21–22
in Social Identity Wheel, 21–22

Racial diversity, 5
Recruitment, 72, 100–101, 131
Reflection, self-, checklist for, 46, 47f–48f, 50, 50f, 151f–154f
Religious/spiritual affiliation, in Social Identity Wheel, 25
Resistance, to program integration, 113–114, 133, 139
Resistant teachers, 55, 56, 58
Respect level of support for multicultural education, 125
Responsive Classroom, 87
Restorative justice, 131
Retraumatizing discussions and videos, 139–140
Ridiculing, communication block of, 35
Robinson, L., 29
Rudge, Leila, 39–40

Sandberg, Sheryl, 19
Sarcasm, 35
Scarbrough, Elizabeth, 81
Schema theory, xv–xvi
School policies, 130–131
Segregation, 63, 65, 118
Self-assessment, with environmental scan scoring guide, 141, 141f, 156f
Self-esteem, xvi
Self-reflection, checklist for, 46, 47f–48f, 50, 50f, 151f–154f
SES, see Socioeconomic status
Sex
 definition of, 23, 24f
 in Social Identity Wheel, 23
Sexual orientation
 definition of, 23, 24f
 in Social Identity Wheel, 23
Sharing, in Morning Meetings, 88
Sharma, Robin, 77
Sliding glass doors, metaphorical, 11–12
S.M.A.R.T. goals, 54–55, 57, 107
Snacks, cultural, 113
Social Action Approach, 124–125
Social identity, see Identities
Social identity theory, xv–xvi
Social Identity Wheel, 20–25, 21f
 at first training workshop, 91
 introduction to, 20–24
Social inequality, 7
Socialization, Cycle of, 115, 116–118, 116f
Socioeconomic status (SES), in Social Identity Wheel, 23
Spiritual affiliation, see Religious/spiritual affiliation

Square, Triangle, Circle activity, 93
Staff
 onboarding new, 141
 ways of increasing diversity of, 100–101, 131
Star Activity, 115
State laws and mandates, 137–138
Status differences, 34
Stereotypes
 in books, 84f
 of generations, 25
Straight, use of term, 92
Strengths, weaknesses, opportunities, and threats (SWOT) evaluation, 135–137, 136f
Strengths-based approach, 86
Structural (transformative) change, 123–132
 multicultural curriculum in, 123–132
 outside classrooms, 130–132
Structural inequality, 7
Structural Reform Stage, 124–125
Structural/Transformation Change rating on Anti-Ism Scale, 72–73, 73t
Subjective language, 27–28
Supervising, 51–58
 adult learning theory in, 45–46
 barriers to, 52
 checklist for self-reflection in, 46, 47f–48f
 vs. coaching, 52, 53
 goals and timing of, 51–52, 51t
 setting professional development goals in, 52–58
"Switch Sides If" game, 89
SWOT evaluation, 135–137, 136f
Symbolic/Compliant Change rating on Anti-Ism Scale, 69–70
Systemic -isms, 142, 143f

Tajfel, H., xv–xvi
Team journals, 94
Textbooks, state laws and mandates on, 138
Throw Me Your Idea activity, 103
Time commitment, in Diversity Workgroups, 98, 102
Ting-Toomey, Stella, 34
Tokenism
 in Anti-Ism Scale, 69, 70
 definition of, 60
 in Diversity Workgroups, 101
Tolerance
 in Anti-Ism Scale, 66–68
 definition of, 67

Tolerance level of support for multicultural education, 125
Tracy, Brian, 111
Training workshops, see Workshops
Transformation Approach, 124–125
Transformative change, see Structural change
Transgender, 23
Trevor Project, 115
Trigger warnings, 140
Triggering discussions and videos, 139–140
Trust, Circle of, 58
Turner, J. C., xv–xvi
Tweet It activity, 94

Uncomfortable, being, 38–39
Upchurch, A., 117

Verbs, action, 78, 80f
Videos
 Hidden Bias, 115, 118–119
 triggering and retraumatizing, 139–140
Visual microaggressions, 132
Volunteers, 94, 97–99
Vulnerability, in community agreements, 90

Websites, 132
WGBH Educational Foundation, 4
White, use of term, 22, 92
Whole-group learning topics, 80–86
Why, defining your, 91
Willingham, A., 27
Windows, metaphorical, 11, 12
Word clouds, 92–93, 93f
Workgroups, see Diversity Workgroups
Workshops, 77–94
 agendas for, 77–86, 94, 95f
 community agreements in, 90–91
 conclusion activities in, 92–94
 defining your why in, 91
 Morning Meetings in, 87–90
 next steps after, 94
 objectives for, 78
 whole-group learning topics for, 77, 80–86
Worthy, L., 23
"Would You Rather" game, 89

Zero-tolerance policies, 131
Zones of comfort, 56–57, 57f, 142